The Entrepreneur's Edge

The Entrepreneur's Edge

ENTREPRENEURIAL THINKING AND THE
MIND/BUSINESS CONNECTION

About half of small businesses fail within five years of startup, and most of the survivors struggle from year to year, not failing, but not really succeeding either. Why do so few succeed? Their "edge" is entrepreneurial thinking and an authentic mind/business connection.

First your mind ... then your business

Alex Alexander

ISBN-13: 9780692524671
ISBN-10: 0692524673
Library of Congress Control Number: 2015920044
Full Spectrum Publishing, Penn Valley, CA

Edited by Melanie Fitch

This book is dedicated to the worldwide network
of Full Spectrum business coaches. They're
talented, big-hearted, and committed.
Their work makes the world
a better place.

Thanks

First and foremost, my life partner, Ali Patricia McKeon, and my daughters Kristen Rachel Alexander and Erin Alexander – each an amazing woman in her own right, and each, in her own way, an inspiration to me – are the light of my life. For them, love, gratitude, admiration, and love again.

My thanks and deepest respects go to Michael Gerber, entrepreneur, business visionary, and author of the best-selling E-Myth books. Michael turned the small business coaching industry on its ear with more innovations than I can count, and through the influence of his books, his public speaking, and his creation of what I think of as "leveraged coaching," has been our industry's foremost pioneer. I worked for him for five years and those years opened up a whole new life for me.

Endless gratitude goes to my teammates, the leaders of Full Spectrum Coaching – Don Farnden, Seth Getz, Lesley Ann Grimoldby, and Curt Rebhan. If we didn't work together, I would still want them as friends. For honesty, integrity, and sheer talent, they have no equal. They are the heart and soul of our coaching business, and the world of business leaders would do well to imitate them.

Table of Contents

Foreword

This book is as much about clear thinking and taking charge of your mind as it is about entrepreneurship. It attempts to bridge the frontier between the academic world of mind/brain science and the down and dirty world of businesses and the entrepreneurs who create them. It wasn't written to be a best seller. It's too "heavy" for that, and not entertaining enough. If you engage it, it makes you think. It makes you work. It makes you admit things about yourself that no normal person wants to admit. It tells you that you may have to make changes that don't feel right, and are awkward. Nobody wants to do any of that.

Not at first.

But when you suspend your disbelief, open up to the possibilities (even if you don't really believe them in the beginning) and dip your toe in the water, you begin to get interesting results. You start seeing things more clearly than those around you. Your decisions begin to get better outcomes than they used to. You have fewer disappointments, and they lose the sting of failure and become learning experiences.

It's my assertion that there are only two paths to business success: entrepreneurial thinking and chance. Entrepreneurial thinking is the reliable path; everything else is a form of chance. An ownership mindset, managerial talent, investment savvy, and workplace/job skills are all important and contribute in significant ways to success, but *only* if guided by entrepreneurial thinking. As you'll see in the pages of this book, entrepreneurial thinking is the advantage – the edge – that leads to sustained success.

Most small business leaders think of themselves as entrepreneurs. Most of them are wrong. True entrepreneurs are a rare breed; more rare than you think. Would-be entrepreneurs are common; a dime a dozen. Lots of people call themselves entrepreneurs simply because they own, manage or invest in a business, but, as you'll see, they're really not. They're owners, managers, and investors, but not entrepreneurs, no matter how truly, how deeply, they believe they are.

Why do I say there are so few true entrepreneurs?

In the USA, the Bureau of Labor Statistics tracks business failures and startups, and over the years, they have consistently found that about half of business startups fail by their fifth year. Not good odds, but not horrible either; it could be worse.

Well, guess what, it *is* worse.

There's a hidden problem that doesn't show up in the statistics, and it's quality of life. Some unknown but very large number of "successful" businesses aren't really successful at all. Yes, they continue to exist, but it's a stressful, life-draining struggle for the people who own and work for them. I can't honestly count those struggling businesses as successful. I don't know the exact numbers, but it's my educated guess that no more than 10% of business startups end up successful, meaning that they provide their leaders and investors with growing, highly profitable businesses that give them satisfaction and contribute to, rather than drag down, their lives.

It doesn't have to be that way, and that's why I've written this book. In its pages, you'll learn about the "mind/business connection" which is the hallmark of a true entrepreneur, one who is capable of creating a lasting, successful business. I'll show you that the vast majority of us have flawed beliefs about businesses and ourselves, conscious and unconscious thinking habits that distort our perception of what's real and what's not, and personality habits that limit our success. And I'll show you what you can do to put your amazing mind to better use by becoming a true entrepreneur and building your own kind of mind/business connection.

In sum, this book offers you a path to success. It's full of things you can use immediately to improve yourself and your business (if you're willing), things designed to shift your thinking (if you're open to new thinking), and things designed to raise your goals and expectations for your business and yourself (if you dare).

Alex Alexander
January 2016
Penn Valley, California

How to Use This Book

There are two ways to read this book: academically and experientially. If you're an academic reader (one who wants to know about the subject, but isn't interested in applying it to him/herself), you'll find some sections tedious. You'll probably skim or skip them. But if you're an experiential reader, one who's interested in using the book to become a better entrepreneur, let me urge you to work your way through it, at a pace that works for you, but thoroughly, one step at a time. If it takes you several weeks to work your way through the book, that's probably a good thing.

This book wasn't designed to be a one-time read. If you read it once, then put it away on your bookshelf or in your digital archives, you're missing much of its value. You'll get more value if you absorb it piecemeal by thinking about and practicing the various parts of it as you encounter them, mastering each part, and then moving on to other parts. Also, the second (and third, and fourth) times you refer to it, you'll find yourself learning things you weren't ready to absorb the first time you read it. And finally, the sections of the book are cumulative, meaning that reading an earlier section, and especially doing the thinking and practice it calls for, prepares you to get the most from the later sections.

With that in mind, I've written this book so you can use it two ways:

1. It's a quick education on entrepreneurial thinking, innovation, and how to develop a successful business.

Read it. Study it. It's actually a short master's degree in small business entrepreneurship. You'll see business development as you've probably never seen it before, in ways that help you understand what business is all about, and especially how to create a business that survives, thrives, and grows.

2. It's a permanent reference that you'll use whenever the need occurs.

- Take it off the shelf or out of your electronic archives once a year to refresh your business savvy.
- Use it to re-motivate yourself when things get stale or overwhelming.
- Look at it when you're planning a new strategy, working on a tricky business problem, launching a new opportunity, training new managers, or any other time you have a business challenge that needs your attention.
- Use it as a business development checklist; especially the chapter on the inner workings of a successful business.

Keep this book handy. You'll find yourself referring to it more often than you might expect. Don't be surprised if you begin to think of it as your "business bible" and refer to it whenever troubles and opportunities arise in your business.

Part One: The Entrepreneur's Mind: What Goes Wrong?

CHAPTER 1

Limiting Beliefs

Five Myths About Business

There are several underlying causes for the abysmal failure rate of small businesses, and they stem from five misunderstandings about businesses and the people who run them.

The problem with these myths, and others I'll reveal in this book, is that they lead to stupid decision-making. And yes, smart people can and do make stupid decisions. A decision not based in reality is a stupid decision. Stupid decisions occasionally work out – a blind squirrel finds a nut now and then, and a stopped clock is right twice a day – but they work out by luck and chance, not by smart thinking.

The whole point about exposing these myths is this: Everything you do as a business leader must be based on the reality of the situation. Not what everyone "knows." Not conventional wisdom. Not belief. Not opinion. Not assumptions. You need facts and reliable information, and when you can't get those (and often you can't) you need rational assumptions, seasoned judgment, and sensible (not emotional) thinking. You need to be grounded in reality, or as close to objective reality as is humanly possible. (For you philosophers out there, yes, there is such a thing as objective reality, but that's a debate for another book.)

Here are the most important five of the many myths about small businesses, and why each myth is dead wrong.

Myth #1: The Business is the Problem

When you hear about the problems of small business people, you hear complaints like these: the economy is lousy, competition is tough, there are too many regulations, things are changing too fast and we can't keep up, there's just too damn much confusion and stress, my employees are lazy, or incompetent, or dishonest, there's just not enough time, and on and on. Small business leaders spend more and more time in their businesses, and less and less time with their families and friends and doing what they really want to do in life. It all comes down to this: "I just can't get this business to work the way it should."

What's Real:

All businesses face similar difficulties: the economy, competition, changes in markets, natural disasters, crime, government regulations, etc. Successful businesses face the same kinds of difficulties as unsuccessful businesses, but the successful leaders find ways to succeed where the losers struggle or fail, and make excuses. Successful business leaders – true entrepreneurs – see these difficulties not as obstacles, but simply as conditions to be recognized and dealt with.

The real (and only) difference between failing businesses and successful businesses is the business leader. The problem for any small business in difficulty can always be traced back to the person, or team, running the business.

If you are a business owner, and your business isn't doing as well as you think it should, the problem isn't the lousy economy, or the competition, or the slow suppliers, or rapidly increasing costs, or employees who are lazy and incompetent. The business isn't the problem; the business leader is the problem, and that's you. To fix the business, you need to fix you.

Myth #2: The Entrepreneurial Myth (Thank You, Michael Gerber)

Michael Gerber was the visionary who, in the 1980s, identified and wrote a best-selling book about what he called "The E-Myth" (short for

"Entrepreneurial Myth"). In Gerber's own words, the E-Myth is this: "...if you understand the technical work of a business, you understand a business that does that technical work." Stated differently: If you know how to do the work of a business, you know how to create and manage a business that does that work. It's wrong, but the belief persists today among most small business managers, and it blinds them to the real possibilities for success, wealth, and better lives.

What's Real:

The *work* of a business requires technical knowledge and skills. Creating a successful business to do that work requires entrepreneurial knowledge, attitudes, and abilities. Small business managers (most of them) are sorely lacking in entrepreneurial abilities; they have the mindset of a jobholder. They mistakenly believe they're entrepreneurs because they are their own bosses, and own their own businesses. They may be managers but they're definitely not entrepreneurs.

By the way, franchise owners aren't entrepreneurs, they're a special kind of manager. Yes, they own and manage a business, but they aren't engaged in business development. There's no creativity, no self-determination, and minimal discretion about how the business grows and is managed. They have the illusion of being their own bosses, but in actuality, they're bound to follow a path of someone else's design. Don't get me wrong, there's nothing wrong with franchising. In fact it's a wonderful way to succeed in business if you can afford the buy-in and can put up with the limitations. However, if you operate a franchise don't kid yourself that you're an entrepreneur, because you're not.

Managers work in businesses and follow the rules. Entrepreneurs create businesses and make up the rules.

Myth #3: Progress is the Same as Success

If you don't know what's possible, small steps forward, or even mere survival can seem like success. But real success is the achievement of your hopes and dreams, not mere survival. For small businesses, it's almost always true that breakthroughs and dramatic leaps forward are not only possible, they're inevitable, but only if you know they're possible, and if you know how to make them happen.

Why does that matter? What's wrong with progress?

Look at it this way: If you've been starving all your life and someone offers you breadcrumbs, you're happy. You have more than you had before, so of course you're happy. Breadcrumbs are progress. But if your eyes are opened and you come to realize that there is a world of plenty, and it's available to you if you know how to get it, then you're no longer happy with breadcrumbs. You have a larger understanding of reality, and a whole new view of "success."

In a way, that's the world of small businesses. Breadcrumbs are the norm, and not many struggling business leaders realize that more is possible. Dreams of abundance are merely dreams of bigger piles of breadcrumbs. When business leaders' eyes are opened to reality, and they come to understand the greater possibilities within their reach, suddenly breadcrumbs don't seem so special.

What's Real:

There's nothing wrong with progress unless it blinds you to the real possibilities. If you expect small steps forward, and small steps make you happy, then your ambitions will be small, your actions will be limited, and your definition of success will be pretty boring. If, on the other hand, you know that much more is achievable – not wishful thinking and fantasy, but real-world results – then you do yourself a disservice by thinking small.

Success beats progress, every time. Progress isn't bad, but success is better. In business, survival is not success. Baby steps are not success. Breakthroughs are success.

Myth #4: Business Development Should Be Simple, Easy, Quick, and Cheap

The problem here is wishful thinking. Small business managers are overworked, stressed, and often confused. It's only natural for them to wish for relief from all that pressure. Consultants, coaches, teachers, and business media all pander to that universal wish by glossing over the true complexity of business, and promising that it's simple, easy, quick, and cheap to create a successful enterprise. Small business managers are only too eager to buy into these ideas. Their false expectation is that all they have to do is find the right process, formula, template, best practice, or trendy secret to success, and then install it in their businesses, and success will follow. Well, success rarely follows, and all too often simple-easy-quick-and-cheap actually makes things worse rather than better.

The false belief is this: All businesses are basically alike, and because a solution worked somewhere, for someone, it will work anywhere, for anyone.

What's Real:

Any situation, any business, is what it is, not what you wish it to be. A business, no matter how small, is a complex organism. *That's* reality.

Businesses, like people, have many similarities, but like human beings, they're dramatically different in many important ways, and each requires its own unique solutions in order to achieve success. Businesses operate in different markets, different locations, have different products and services and cost structures. Business managers have different personalities, strengths, weaknesses, preferences, and strategies.

Also, businesses and the conditions they face change over time, and their managers also change and grow over time. Solutions that work now won't work the same in the future. Cookie-cutter solutions (even the few that work in the beginning) don't adapt over time but instead become outdated and part of the problem rather than the solution.

When simple, easy, quick, and cheap gets the job done, then that's what you should do. When the situation is more complex and requires thought, creativity, and, yes, complexity, then *that's* what you should do. Glossing over the underlying complexity of a situation in order to give the appearance of simplicity, wanting a task that is inherently difficult to be easy, and looking for a quick path to an innately long-term result, are all ways of avoiding reality and giving in to wishful thinking.

Simple isn't necessarily bad, and when simple solutions really do work, they should be used. Simple is better when simple works. The problem is that, more often than not, the simple solution really doesn't work. Not if the goal is success rather than failure or miserable survival.

In business, reality isn't often simple, easy, quick, or cheap. You have to deal with the situation as it is; deal with reality, or pay the price.

Myth #5: The Path to Success is Trial and Error (an Unconscious Myth)

This isn't really a myth because it's not a conscious belief, it's a mind-set. It's the way most small business leaders move into their futures.

Trial and error is just what it says. You try something, and if it doesn't work, you try something else, and you keep trying. The belief is that eventually, if you keep at it, you'll discover the secret to success.

One form of trial and error is the "formula" approach to business development. Formulas include templates, practices, academic theories, seven (or three, or five, or whatever number) steps to success, and they're all forms of imitation (they're also forms of simple, easy, quick, and cheap). It feels like you're avoiding the perils of trial and error because you're using a "proven" method, but all you're doing is trying the formula in your business to see if it works, and then changing it, and changing it again when it doesn't work. It's still trial and error.

What's Real:

Trial and error is a path of never ending struggle and half-baked results. It's a path of randomness, in which success is more a matter of luck than intention.

The trial and error process – trying something you've dreamed up, or a formula that you've learned about – is falsely encouraging because, in most cases, some bits of it will work even though most of it doesn't. You notice the bits that work, and downplay what doesn't. You made a bit of progress, and it feels like you're making headway, because you actually *have* made a bit of headway. Isn't that breadcrumbs again? If you want breakthroughs rather than "a little bit of headway," trial and error won't get the job done for you. It can occasionally work, but the odds are long against you. You try something, and if it doesn't work, you try something else, and you keep trying until you either get it right or you run out of money. You can guess what happens to most small businesses.

There will always be some trial and error, even in the best-run businesses. But entrepreneurial thinking gets you to success with less trial, less error, and therefore less stress, less misery, and *much* more satisfaction. You'll see in this book how that happens.

If you're satisfied with random results, and you're willing to depend on luck, then trial and error is your strategy.

CHAPTER 2

Habits of Mind and How They Work

What Are Habits of Mind?

Your habits of mind are automatic patterns of thinking and being, and they operate mostly unconsciously, usually hidden from your awareness. Some of them are inborn, but you develop most of them as you live your life, beginning at the moment of birth (some say earlier) and continuing to the moment of death (some say beyond). Your habits of mind enable you to cope with the world in which you live, your relationships with other people, and the situations that crop up in your life. You start with an inborn set of rudimentary habits, and as you mature, more habits are conditioned into you by your parents, the ever-widening circle of people in your life, and your responses to your needs and experiences.

It's useful to think of two kinds of mental habits, and I'll devote a chapter in this book to each of them:

Habits of **thinking** are beliefs, mental models, intuitions, the ways we make assumptions, and other patterns of conscious and unconscious thinking.

Habits of **being** are personality and character traits. They're the answers to the question, "What kind of person am I?" They're described with words like, courageous, generous, optimistic, rebellious, shy, aggressive, easygoing, honest, impulsive, etc.

Brain scientists are currently leaning toward an understanding of habits, including habits of mind, as bundles of neural activity, which get triggered, and then automatically run their course. It's sort of like a computer program. You first initiate a command of some kind by pushing a button, entering a code, or setting some kind of numerical parameter. The command starts the program (triggers it) and then the program goes through its step-by-step process until it completes its activity.

You couldn't do without your habits of mind, and you wouldn't want to, but sometimes they get in your way. Difficulties arise when your habits aren't appropriate or effective for the situations in which you find yourself. They become problematic when they block clarity and rational thinking. When that happens, and it happens a lot, entrepreneurial thinking is impossible.

This chapter lays the foundation for a general understanding of habits of mind and how sometimes they can be dysfunctional.

I've taken great pains to make sure everything in this book is consistent with what's known of mind/brain operation these days, but I'm not going to regurgitate much of that because, like driving an automobile, you don't have to know the physics and electronics of a car in order to drive it, you simply have to know how to manage the controls. In the same way, you don't have to know mind/brain science in order to "drive" your mind. You only have to know how to make it work the way you want it to.

Still, you need to understand some basics, so let me cover some things that'll help you learn how to "drive" your mind better so that the entrepreneur within you (the true entrepreneur, not the pretender) can create your mind/business connection and get you where you want to be.

Associations, Interconnectedness, Interdependency, and Enormous Complexity...All of It Beneath the Surface

We all know the metaphor of a duck swimming on a pond; the duck appears calm and placid above the water, while its feet are churning wildly beneath the surface. Well, that's your mind. Above the surface, in your conscious mind, things seem relatively straightforward, while below the surface in your unconscious mind, an enormous number of connections and impulses are wildly churning here and there, at incredible speeds, and with even more incredible complexity. You're not even aware of them, although you're completely dependent upon them for your very survival and sanity.

I bring up the subject of complexity and interconnectedness for a reason, and this is something you need to grasp, because it is one of the keys for learning how to guide and direct your own unconscious thinking. One of the most miraculous things your brain does with all of its complexity is to create associations.

Every moment you live your life and think your thoughts, your brain is creating associations, and these associations are assembled from all of your sensory perceptions, your conscious and unconscious thoughts, memories, emotions; anything that is detected or generated by your conscious and unconscious mind. A child at a circus doesn't simply see some circus acts and eat some cotton candy. She experiences a barrage of smells, noises, tactile sensations, and tastes. She has a flood of thoughts and impressions. Her emotions are tugged this way and that, from delight to fear to bewilderment, and more. All those perceptions, and much more, are associated with her circus experience. In later years, the smell of cotton candy, or the sound of a calliope, or the whinny of a horse, or a particular sharp tone of voice that sounds vaguely like the circus ringmaster, or any one of hundreds (even thousands) of impressions will bring back a mental version of the entire circus experience because they're all linked in her mind by associations. The more intense the emotions of the event, the more lasting and intense will be the associations. Ask any veteran of the Vietnam War what happens when she/he hears a helicopter. Ask any heart attack survivor what happens when she/he smells a certain kind of plastic (the kind that oxygen hoses are made of). Ask anyone what happens when you say the word "mother."

Anything that ever happened to you had a context, there were sounds, sights, smells, textures, tastes, thoughts, emotions, and intuitions happening, as well as other multi-layered associations connected with them. The more intense the experience – intensity has a lot to do with emotion – the more deeply imbedded the associations.

It's through associations (and purposeful creation of unconscious habits of mind; more about that later) that we can bring conscious intention, rather than automatic reaction, to our unconscious minds and much of our conscious decision-making.

Speaking of the unconscious mind...

Your Unconscious Mind Is In Charge

The unconscious mind is something we don't pay much attention to because it's invisible to us. It operates automatically, and with blinding speed. It learns when we don't know it's learning, and sometimes it learns the wrong things and feeds us the wrong information. We don't control it, although we can learn to. It's the source, by far, of most of our mental processes.

Bad news: the dominance of your unconscious mind keeps your entrepreneurial thinking blocked.

Dominance of your unconscious mind?

Really?

Yes, really.

Did you know that when you make a conscious decision, your unconscious mind had already made that decision something like three-tenths of a second earlier? Decisions are made by the unconscious mind, and then either carried out or negated by the conscious mind. Mind/brain scientists have measured both the sequence – first unconscious, then conscious – and the elapsed time, about three-tenths of a second between the instant your unconscious mind makes a decision and the instant your conscious mind registers it. Even when we feel that our conscious minds are directing our thoughts and actions, in actuality we're mainly driven by our unconscious minds. The *un*conscious mind is the leader. The conscious mind is the follower. It doesn't *feel* like that, but that's the way it is. Neuroscience consistently proves and re-proves it.

Fortunately, your conscious mind has the ability take charge and put itself in the leadership position either by negating unconscious decisions or by deliberately and consciously creating unconscious habits of mind involved in decision-making. Yes, you can reshape your unconscious thinking. That's critical because the *conscious* mind is the driver of entrepreneurship, and only when the conscious mind is in the leadership position can true entrepreneurial thinking emerge.

Let's examine unconscious thinking a bit more closely, and you'll see what I mean.

Did you know that 95% (probably much more) of your thinking and perceiving happens unconsciously? It's true, and it's a good thing, because if you had to think and do everything consciously, you'd go nuts. Some things, actually *most* things, are best left to our unconscious mental processes, especially routine, repetitive activities like walking, reading, chewing, and thousands of other activities. On the other hand, some things need to be dealt with consciously because they're new, risky, or important, and because, sometimes, the unconscious mind encounters contradictions and paradoxes, and the conscious mind has to step in to resolve them.

First, if you've never thought about it, take a moment to convince yourself that most of your mental processes are unconscious.

Take the simple act of reading – what you're doing right now. When you first started reading as a toddler, you laboriously (and consciously) learned the alphabet. After a while you could recite your ABCs automatically and unconsciously. Then you learned the sounds of the letters, consciously. After a while, the sounds were automatically associated with the letters and you didn't have to think consciously about them any more. Then you learned about spelling: C-A-T. Then sentences, paragraphs, and ultimately whole books. Now, when you read, do you think about the letters? The sounds? Are you aware of sentence structure? Do you have to translate words into ideas? No. You do it all automatically and unconsciously. What you do consciously is think about the ideas and images that your unconscious mind extracted from the letters, words, punctuation, paragraphs, and pages. When you read a book, or a newspaper, or a product label, your unconscious mind does all the hard work so your conscious mind will be free to deal with the ideas your unconscious mind extracted from ink spots on a page or pixels on a screen.

What happens when you come upon an unfamiliar word or bad grammar in your reading? It pops you out of unconscious thinking into conscious thinking, doesn't it? At least momentarily. Then you decide what to do about it; you can look up the unfamiliar word, figure out its meaning from the context, or simply ignore it. The same kind of thing happens when you're driving your car. You're buzzing along, listening to the radio or talking with a friend while your driving is taken care of automatically by your unconscious mind. But when something unexpected occurs, say another driver swerves in front of you, you pop out of unconscious thinking, and your conscious mind instantly takes over to cope with the situation. When the situation becomes routine again, you ease back into unconscious driving.

Your actions are still driven by your unconscious mind but your conscious mind becomes aware of what's happening, and has the ability to interrupt the unconscious action if necessary. For instance, you might have the unconscious urge to swerve your own car to avoid the reckless driver in front of you, but swerving would put you into even greater danger from the cars on either side, so your conscious mind holds your course steady and slows down, overriding the unconscious urge to turn to the side, into greater danger.

Mind/brain scientists will quickly tell you that it's not as simple as I've described, because your conscious and unconscious thinking are continuously interactive, not separate thought mechanisms. They're right, of course, but the point is that, when the situation calls for it, two things happen: Firstly, your awareness – your conscious mind – puts its attention on the situation, and secondly, your conscious thinking can alter your unconscious decision making. Your conscious mind has the ability to influence your unconscious thinking, and it's this ability that gives you the power to consciously shape your unconscious mind. Later in the book, I'll show you how to do it to reshape dysfunctional habits of mind.

A lot of your unconscious thinking was learned _un_consciously. For instance, most of us can tell when someone is sad. How did you learn to detect that people are sad, or happy, or stressed, or angry? You learned from experience, by seeing human behavior and unconsciously picking up little clues here and there. The older you got, the better you became at detecting people's moods, or any of thousands of other things that you don't think about, you just "know". In his best-selling book *Blink*, Malcolm Gladwell describes this process of unconscious learning much better than I can.

By the way, don't make the mistake of believing that your thinking is either conscious or unconscious. Your brain isn't a toggle switch that's in either the conscious or the unconscious position. Your unconscious thinking is always feeding impressions to your conscious mind, and your conscious mind is always deciding what to do about them, and feeding that thinking back into your unconscious mind in an endless loop (actually, millions of loops). Even such "conscious" activities as conversing with friends depends upon the unconscious mind's ability to detect and decipher sounds and deliver their meaning to your conscious mind. You consciously deal with the ideas, while your unconscious mind is receiving sound signals, comparing them with your mental models, adding whatever emotional component it finds appropriate, and feeding its conclusions to your conscious mind.

When things are routine, non-threatening, and generally meet with your expectations, your unconscious thinking dominates your actions. But when you're surprised, threatened, or conflicted, your conscious thinking supersedes your unconscious thinking until the situation is resolved. Your unconscious mind is still cranking away, and most of your mental activity continues to be of the unconscious sort. Your conscious thinking is still taking in all the impressions provided by your unconscious thinking, reacting to your beliefs and mental models about the way the world works, and in general still depends on the unconscious mind for a sense of right and wrong, expectations about what will happen next, and for the emotional responses that give meaning to it all. In other words, even though your conscious thinking is fully engaged, that conscious thinking is still shaped by your unconscious mind. That's how your conscious thinking works, and will continue to work until you learn how to put it *truly* in charge.

Beware! Your unconscious mind (and mine) can, and does, deceive you (and me).

Let me pass on to you a few brief examples of what the experts in the field of brains and minds tell us about our unconscious thinking, and a few of the ways it can lead us astray. You'll see later why this is so extremely important, and you'll learn some techniques for making your unconscious mind work for you, rather than you for it.

- If we like something, or if it stimulates pleasant emotions, our unconscious minds perceive it as factual, accurate, correct, and right, whether or not it actually is. If we're aware of this effect, our conscious minds can override such false impressions, but most of us don't know about it. So, when our unconscious minds make us "feel" like something is right, even when it's not, we accept it as right.

- If we're familiar with an idea, our unconscious minds also perceive it as correct and good, again, whether or not it actually is. The same is true of repetition of ideas. The more they are repeated, and if we have no preconceived opinions about them, the more we perceive them as correct and right. Advertisers and propagandists all know this. Again, if we know about it, our conscious minds can overcome this dysfunctional effect.

- If an idea is easy to grasp – simple, clear, brief – our unconscious minds perceive it as correct and right, whether or not it is so, compared with a more complex, harder to understand idea. That's why people so often take the simpler idea as true, and ignore or pooh-pooh the reality of a more complex idea. By the way, Occam's Razor – the principle that the simplest of two or more competing theories is preferable – is a falsehood. Neither simplicity nor complexity makes something true, reality is what it is, whether simple or complex.

- If people we like and/or trust tell us something, our unconscious minds perceive it as correct and right, unless we have other preconceptions, and even then we might override our preconceptions if our faith in the person telling us is strong enough.

- Our unconscious minds act as if the information in our memory and experience is all the information there is on a subject, even if we are incompletely and incorrectly informed. The unconscious mind also has a "coherence" function; it has the ability to build coherent stories with the information, associations, and experiences available to it. It then, unconsciously, makes evaluations and draws conclusions that seem sensible and real, and finally presents the results to our conscious minds in the form of impressions and judgments. The phenomenon was observed by Nobel Prize winner Daniel Kahneman, who called it "WYSIATI," the acronym for "what you see is all there is." WYSIATI and the coherence function cause our minds to jump to conclusions based on limited, often insufficient evidence, and it causes us to have unwarranted certainty about our conclusions, even when they're wrong.

- At any point in time, we have the ability to override our unconscious thinking with our conscious thinking (except for the autonomous bodily functions, and even they sometimes yield to conscious manipulation).

This is just a sampling of what has been discovered about the workings of our unconscious minds. There's a lot more, and more is being discovered every day.

In summary, a huge amount of your thinking is done unconsciously, and most of your conscious thinking is shaped by your unconscious mind, but the conscious mind has the ability, if you're aware enough, to take charge.

Why is the dominance of the unconscious mind so critical, and why is it so important that the conscious mind take the leadership position in your thought processes? It's because, more than anything else, your unconscious mind shapes your perception of what's real and what isn't, what's the truth, and what isn't. When your sense of what's real is distorted, your thinking is distorted, and when your thinking is distorted, your decisions and actions will be ineffective.

Reality A and Reality B: There are Two Truths for Everything

For every situation, there is an actual, factual reality; something exists or something happened. That's what I call "Reality A," and it's the objective, actual reality (the factual reality) of the world outside of our minds.

Separately from Reality A, there is our internal experience of that reality. That's what I call "Reality B," which is our subjective, inner perception. They're not always the same. In fact, they're never the same because one is external and real in the world outside of our skulls, and the other is our perception of it, an idea within our minds, what some have called an "internal representation" of reality.

Reality A is what it is.

Reality B is what we perceive it to be.

A lot of the struggle of life is the attempt to create an internal understanding, Reality B, in our minds that matches up with the facts of Reality A. Many problems in life happen when we get it wrong, when Reality B doesn't match up with Reality A.

Reality B is a lot like a road map. It's a representation of something in the world, but it's not that thing. A map of the road from home to work is not the same as the actual road from home to work, but if the map faithfully represents that road, then it's a very useful thing. If the map is in error, it's worse than useless. It misleads us. It lies to us. And any decisions or actions we take based on an erroneous map will lead us astray.

Within our minds, our internal reality, Reality B, seems to be the one-and-only actual reality. We don't know when it's in error unless we know how to engage our conscious minds and force ourselves to become aware that our internal reality is different from the external reality.

Why does Reality B stray from the factuality of Reality A? It's because our minds process and interpret the factual data that our senses detect. We process and reshape it based on our beliefs and expectations, and on the way our minds work.

For example, the eyes and ears report facts: a loud noise, a flash of light, and the direction from which they come. The mind, based on experience, what has been learned in the past (and some beliefs) interprets these factual observations and concludes "thunder and lightning." But that's not all that's attached to the experience. A thousand years ago, part of the experience was fear because it was believed that thunder was an expression of the anger of the gods, and the ancient observer might have prayed or made a sacrifice to appease those gods. Reality A was thunder and lightning. Reality B was angry gods. Fast forward to today. Because of today's education and prevailing beliefs, the modern observer still perceives "thunder and lightning," but the experience also includes thoughts about clouds, wind, and depending on the individual's education, associated ideas about static electricity and electric currents heating up the air so quickly that a sonic boom is created. If there is fear, it's not fear of the gods' anger, but anxiety about getting wet, or, if close enough, fear of a lightning strike.

Thunder and lightning are what they are, they're factual, but the minds of observers can generate radically different inner perceptions of them. Reality A (the factual reality), because of our internal processing, can give rise to a different and distorted Reality B (the experiential reality).

Here's another example:

You're in a courtroom. Two eyewitnesses – young men in their early twenties, friends, who were walking together – saw two men fighting. They observed the assault from the same vantage point, at the same time. They witnessed one and only one event, one and only one Reality A. Neither witness knew or had any connection with either the defendant or the plaintiff, so there were no personal biases to muddy the waters. But look at the differences in their Reality Bs. Witness #1 said, "I saw the defendant attack the plaintiff for no reason." Witness #2 said, "I saw the plaintiff take a swing at the defendant, and the defendant was simply protecting himself."

Again, a single Reality A gives rise to different and contradictory Reality Bs. There was one and only one actual event, but the minds of the two witnesses contained contradictory perceptions.

My point, and forgive me for being Captain Obvious, is that we all create mental models of reality; we have to, we're built that way. Usually our mental models serve us well, but often, for all kinds of reasons, our models can be, and often are, flawed, even though we completely and sincerely, consciously and unconsciously, believe them to be "the" reality.

Here's the problem: We base our actions on the internal experience of Reality B, not the factuality of Reality A, because Reality B is all our minds know. Our minds fully believe that B *is* A. And, when our internal realities are flawed, which they often are, we make mistakes, and our actions fall short of our expectations or fail completely. The more complex the reality, the less we understand it, and the more flawed our Reality B is. The consequences can be trivial (does it really matter if some people still think thunder is an expression of angry gods?), or enormously consequential (Adolph Hitler's Reality B killed millions, and Martin Luther King Jr.'s Reality B made millions of lives better).

Reality B matters. A lot. When Reality B reflects the factuality of the world, it leads to success, happiness, and leadership that creates widespread well-being. When it doesn't track with factuality, it leads to mistakes (sometimes catastrophic mistakes) and widespread misery.

So, it's critical – *critical!* – either that your Reality B is a fair representation of Reality A, or that when it's not, you can admit to not knowing, rather than insisting on a flawed Reality B. Often, if not always, "I don't know" is a far better position to take than the certainty of a false Reality B.

So, the all-important question for you is "How can I know when my Reality B is flawed or incomplete?" Even more importantly, "How can I make sure that my Reality B is as close to the real-world Reality A as possible?" That's what the next few chapters are all about.

CHAPTER 3

Habits of Thinking and the Dozen Distortions

Habits of Thinking

Why don't we always see the world as it really is? Why is our Reality B often flawed or incomplete? It's because we see what we expect to see, what we want to see, what someone else tells us to see, what we saw before, or what we believe we should see. We interpret what we see, most often unconsciously, based on the ways we have learned to think – our habits of thinking – over the course of our lives. The mind/brain experts call this conditioning, and it shapes both our conscious and unconscious thinking. In other words, our *perception* of reality is distorted by all manner of habits of thinking which have become a part of our minds over the years. And then, what we *perceive* as reality, accurately or not, is what we deal with as if it were *true* reality.

For instance:

A police officer sees a young man running from the scene of a crime, assumes he's the culprit, and arrests the young man. In reality, the young man had nothing to do with the crime and was merely running to catch a bus. The police officer, not paying attention to the bus, made a wrong assumption because of unconscious habits of thinking that were based on his years of experience. Normally that experience serves the police officer well, but this time it didn't. The officer "filtered" what he saw, created a distorted, inaccurate Reality B, and acted on that perception, believing his perception to be the actual reality. In the mind of the officer, the young man *was* the criminal, but in reality, he wasn't. Reality B didn't match Reality A.

Another for instance:

In a recent political campaign in the USA, one of the leading candidates, known for her tough-mindedness and icy demeanor, was moved to tears when responding to a question from a reporter. Because it was such a departure from her normal behavior, it was widely reported in the press. One television commentator said the candidate was disgusting and phony, although a convincing actress, because she was pretending to be deeply moved in order to be more sympathetic to the voters. "Crying for votes" said the commentator, contemptuously. Another commentator said the candidate, for the first time in public, displayed her passion and commitment by revealing the depth of her caring. No one, except the candidate herself (and maybe not even she), knows the reality behind her emotional response. However, the two commentators, and millions of others, created in their minds perceptions of reality, and they'll cast their votes on the basis of those mental models. Again, Reality B didn't match up with Reality A.

You can see how people who unconsciously distort reality through their habits of thinking put themselves in a position to create false realities, and then behave as if their false realities were true.

The Dozen Distortions – Twelve Habits That Can Distort Your Thinking, and What to Do About Them

There are scores, maybe even hundreds, of different habits of thinking we use to screen and interpret reality. In my experience there are a dozen of them that seem to be the most common and create most of the conscious and unconscious distortions of reality that we observe in the world of small businesses and the "entrepreneurs" who run them. Yes, these habits help streamline our thinking by making it quicker and more efficient, but they can lead us astray when they cause us to jump to unwarranted conclusions, simplify the unsimplifiable, and make flawed assumptions about people and situations. Let me first introduce you to these twelve habits of thinking, which I call the "dozen distortions." Later in this chapter I'll get into their details.

The Dozen Distortions

*A dozen habits of thinking that can, if you're not
paying attention, distort your perception of reality*

Limiting Beliefs – When flawed beliefs get in your way

Generalization and Simplification – When you generalize and
simplify the reality out of a situation

Cause and Effect – When timing and coincidence are liars, and
assumptions lead you astray

Either/Or – When you ignore the spectrum of possibilities, and
assume phony dichotomies

WYSIATI (what you see is all there is) **and Blind Spots** – When
there's more to the story that you need to know

Coherence and Pattern Recognition – Making sense of nonsense
(even when it really is nonsense) and perceiving things that
aren't really there

Expectations, Selective Perception, and the Confirmation Bias –
Reality isn't always what you expect it to be

Emotions – What's important? But is it real?

Projection and the "Me-Bias" – *Your* reality isn't *my* reality. Are
you really as good (or bad) as you think you are?

Focus Blindness and Stress – Your unconscious mind has a mind
of its own, and it doesn't always see what's there to be seen.

Conventional Wisdom, Myths, & Experts – What's right? What's
wrong? Who really knows?

The Tyranny of Experience – Is the past really a guide to the future? Is your internal experience real?

None of these habits of thinking are inherently good or bad, effective or ineffective. We have them because they're useful to us. But sometimes they're not.

Curing the Dozen Distortions – Awareness and The Two-Question Habit

Creating Awareness

In the following pages, I'm going to ask you to read, carefully and attentively, about each of the dozen distortions and to imagine yourself experiencing each of the distortions, even if you believe you're not likely ever to encounter one. By doing this, you'll be "priming" yourself to be aware when a distortion may be happening to you so that you can consciously avoid it. Awareness is the necessary first step. You can't avoid a distortion if you don't even know it's happening to you.

"Priming" is a complex function of the mind. Brain science proves that when your unconscious mind has been exposed to an idea, you're likely to think and behave in alignment with that idea. The form of priming that's useful in this case is this: By reading and thinking about each of the dozen distortions, you prime yourself to become more aware of them as they occur in real life and in real time. When you're aware, you can do something to shift your thinking in order to avoid the distortion. It's "self-priming" and you'll see it again later in this book.

The more attention you put to understanding the dozen distortions and how they play out in your own mind, the more thoroughly you'll be priming yourself to be aware of them, and to eliminate the flawed thinking they create.

By the way, most of us don't believe we distort reality, and that itself is an example of how we distort reality. You may have a bit of difficulty suspending your disbelief, but it's important to be at least open to the slight possibility that you might – just might – occasionally be guilty of distorted thinking.

In short, keep an open mind, and imagine yourself experiencing each distortion as you read about it.

Eliminating the Distortions – the Two-Question Habit

When you've primed yourself to be aware, what can you do about the distortion? You have to create a new habit of thinking, a habit that causes you to want to understand the situation better and to be open to all the possibilities. That, in turn, will stock your unconscious mind with more and better information, and enable its coherence function to come up with a Reality B that's a much closer match with Reality A. You do that by asking yourself two questions, and then answering each to the best of your ability. The questions are:

What's Reality A?
What are the facts? What do you *know* is the actual reality outside of your mind (Reality A) and, separately, what is the product of your opinion or interpretation (Reality B)? What do you believe that could be questioned?

Initially, when you ask this question, it'll be hard to distinguish between Reality A and Reality B because all your life you've been conditioned to perceive and depend upon Reality B as if it were the actual reality rather than an internal perception. But with practice you'll not only get good at it, you'll learn automatically to distinguish between them.

What are the possibilities?
What else do I need to know about the situation? What are the other possibilities, even if they're highly unlikely? How would someone else see the situation?

Your mindset when asking yourself these questions is important. You'll need to adopt the mindset of an objective third party, someone other than yourself. In other words, see yourself and your thinking from the point of view of someone who's not involved. It's tricky at first because our minds want to justify what we "know" rather than challenge it or see it differently. So resist the temptation to justify what you think is true, and dig deeper to see if it really is true or not.

At first, consciously asking yourself these two questions will feel awkward and slow, like all new habits, but stick with it because it'll gradually establish itself as an automatic, instant, and, yes, unconscious, habit of mind. After a while – probably several days, maybe a week or so – you'll no longer even have to think about the questions because your mind will no longer need them. You'll have generated the habit of making sure you've seen reality the way it is by automatically increasing the range of possibilities that come to mind and by having the automatic urge to understand the situation as thoroughly as possible.

At that point it will no longer be the "two-question" habit, it will be a natural inclination to be aware of all possibilities, and to be curious about them.

The Dozen Distortions Up Close and Personal

With that preparation behind us, let's look closely at each of the dozen distortions. Remember, for each distortion, it's important to go through the three-step process:

1. Read about each distortion carefully.
2. Remember, or imagine, that you have experienced that particular distortion. Stay objective, as if you were merely an observer.
3. Ask and answer the two questions to expand your understanding of that situation, and to expose yourself to a broader range of possibilities.

Limiting Beliefs

Belief that something can't be done, someone can't be persuaded, that you lack some talent or skill, that the odds are against you, that it's too hard to start a new business, that you'll make a fool of yourself speaking to a large group, that the risk of [whatever] is too great, and on and on, limit your effectiveness. The belief might be true, it might be self-fulfilling, or it might just be hogwash.

There are also such things as enabling beliefs: the belief that something *can* be done, someone *can* be persuaded, that you *have* a needed talent or skill, that the odds are in your favor, that you *can* start a new business, that you'll do a *great* job speaking to a large group, that the risk of [whatever] is minimal, and again, on and on.

Limiting beliefs and enabling beliefs aren't just a matter of, as the saying goes, "If you think you can, or if you think you can't, you're right." If they were, you would only have to believe to make something possible. It's only when the belief reflects reality or when the belief is so strong that it leads to effective behavior, that it leads to effectiveness and success (enabling beliefs) or ineffectiveness and failure (limiting beliefs). Belief alone accomplishes nothing. Rational belief, followed by *effective behavior*, leads to success. And by "rational belief" I mean belief that is consistent with Reality A.

That's why affirmations, false bravado, "positive thinking," and other attempts at creating enabling beliefs so often lead to frustration, embarrassment, and ultimately failure. You say and think the right things, but somewhere within you, consciously or unconsciously, if you don't really believe them, or if they're not realistic, you won't be able to make these wishes a reality.

In summary, when there is no congruence between your beliefs and reality, the beliefs will be limiting. When the beliefs dovetail with reality, and you really do believe them both consciously and unconsciously, they will be enabling beliefs.

Let me emphasize two forms of limiting beliefs that bedevil most of us:

Self-Perceptions

Self-perception is your conscious, and especially your unconscious, sense of yourself. Unconscious? Yes. Your unconscious sense of yourself, probably even more than your conscious self-image, impacts your effectiveness, and therefore contributes to your success or lack of it. But because it's unconscious, it can have a hidden impact on you.

Here are some examples that illustrate how self-perceptions can shape behavior, not always for the best.

Ted comes from a poor family. He remembers that his mother would never go to an upscale restaurant, not even when he offered to take her for Mother's Day or her birthday. She used to say, "I don't belong in a place like that." [The mother's self-image was that of a "lower class" person without the necessary standing and social skills to behave appropriately in "upper class" situations.]

What a disaster. My boss, Jack, and I went to our first working meeting with a new client. We were meeting the CEO of [a Fortune 500 company]. Jack walked in like he owned the place, and started taking charge from the first minute. You could see the client's face turn to stone. Man, was I embarrassed. [Jack's actual self-image was that of a pretender. He often worried that his clients might discover that he was merely an Average Joe who, by luck, had reached a position of influence and power. To cover up his sense of inferiority, he tried to act like "the smartest guy in the room"; someone who was a take-charge mover and shaker, and who automatically commanded the respect of even the most powerful executives. Because it wasn't consistent with reality, it was never authentic, and the people around him could sense it.]

Can you believe it? I offered Manny a promotion into Sales from Market Research with great pay, a title, responsibility, an expense account, and even a company car. He said no! When I asked why, he said, "I'm a numbers guy, not a salesman. I can't do that kind of work." It's a shame because he has the ability. You should see him win over skeptical clients when he presents his market research reports. [Manny's self-image was exactly what he said it was, in spite of the fact that he had demonstrated to others his persuasive skills.]

Sharon is a natural; three days on the job and she's already a hero. We were about to lose our biggest customer to a competitor who offered a lowball price. Sharon overheard me worrying about it and asked if she could try to turn him around. You should have seen her. She's only three years out of college, but you'd have thought she was a twenty-year veteran. Within a half-hour she put together a service package that brought the customer back, and she didn't even have to cut our price! [Sharon has the self-image of a winner. She believes, and experience has supported her belief, that she can turn around even the most difficult of situations.]

I don't back down from anyone! If you give me a hard time, be prepared for trouble. [This person believes himself to be a forceful, intimidating person who will prevail in most situations, and who will be a problem for those who oppose him.]

The smartest person in the room is Rebecca, but you wouldn't know it. She never speaks up in meetings, and you have to pry opinions and rec-ommendations out of her. But when you do, she always has something worthwhile to contribute. [Rebecca's self-mage is that of a worker bee who has no leadership potential. She knows she's smart, but see's herself as a person who is not respected or listened to by others. In truth, she is highly respected, but her self-perception focuses on the very few instances in which she spoke up, but in which her ideas were not accepted, leav-ing her feeling foolish and inept. Those few instances loom large in her mind, giving rise to a false perception of herself, or more accurately, a self-fulfilling perception.]

Your self-perceptions don't have to be positive or negative. They sim-ply have to be accurate, based on reality, not on a desire to impress your-self or anyone else.

Self-perception should be consistent with your true nature, other-wise, you'll take on tasks for which you're not well suited, or give the appearance of being a "phony" when your behavior doesn't match your assertions about yourself, or resent others when they describe you in ways that seem wrong to you. Basically, an honest, accurate self-image supports effective behavior.

I'm well aware of the prevailing belief that you should "fake it until you make it," in other words, act a certain way, and in time you'll become that way. For instance, take on a positive attitude even if you don't feel positive, and keep doing it. The theory is that eventually, with attention and repetition, you'll actually become innately positive and the habit of mind of being positive will become ingrained within you. But the unconscious mind can be tricky. Faking it until you make it only works if you actually believe it, or are at least consciously and unconsciously open to the possibility. If you truly disbelieve it, even unconsciously, you'll initially "act" the part, and with repetition, instead of integrating the habit of *being* positive, you'll integrate the habit of *acting* positive, without actually becoming positive. The behavior of *appearing* positive will become habitual, but the actual personality trait of *being* positive won't. Do you see the difference? Acting shapes your outward behavior, but not your thinking, but an innate positive attitude shapes everything about you.

The unconscious mind is complex and subtle. And *very* smart. It knows when you're faking it. As you'll see when I show you how to reshape your ineffective habits of mind, it's important to create new habits that are compatible with who you are, so that the resulting new habits will be authentic. If they're not authentically you, they won't shift your thinking, and your old mental habits will persist. You may look outwardly the way you want to look, but inwardly you won't really change. Yet at a conscious level, you'll think you have. In actuality, all you'll have done is to create a new behavioral habit – faking it until you make it, but never quite making it. While your outward behavior may shift a bit, your unconscious thinking remains in place.

Here's an example of someone whose self-perception changed for the better. Let's call him Jason.

Jason struggled for a decade and a half in the banking industry. He had an MBA from a top-ranked school and great leadership training from his military experience. His self-image was that of a person with tremendous upward potential, a corporate achiever who would go far. He was described as brilliant, creative, and resourceful. But his performance evaluations were mediocre, and his promotions few and far between. Eventually, he was laid off, and landed a job as a management consultant, where he did better, yet still didn't succeed as he thought he should. Ultimately, quite by accident, he was offered a position as an adjunct professor at a respected second-tier university. He loves it, and he's good at it. He's thriving. The academic environment, plus the opportunity to do ground breaking research, tapped precisely into his strengths, and gave him a greater sense of accomplishment and fulfillment than he had ever had before.

Jason's self-perception was a false one – a distortion of reality – and it led him to make poor choices and career decisions, until, by accident, he fell into exactly the right career path for him. He could have made much more productive use of fifteen years of his life if he had had an accurate self-perception during that time.

The challenge is to bring your unconscious self-perceptions into your conscious awareness, and to be rigorously honest with yourself *about* yourself.

Persistence of Belief

The majority of people, even when proven wrong about a firmly held opinion, will persist in believing the opinion, especially if the opinion is based on personal experience, a trusted source of information, or a strong desire. Psychologists have documented this effect, and you have undoubtedly seen it in others (we rarely see it in ourselves).

For example, take the case of generic aspirin. Millions of people buy name brand aspirin such as Bayer or Anacin, but generic unbranded aspirin costs a third to a half less *for exactly the same product.* Try to convince the brand loyalists that the generic aspirin is exactly the same, show them studies, show them the ingredient labels on the packages, they still insist that branded aspirin is better and worth the added cost. If you're one of those people, you're undoubtedly shaking your head at my stupidity as you read this paragraph.

Persistence of belief creates two kinds of problems for you. Your own persistence of belief can lead you to make faulty decisions. You need to make a conscious practice of keeping your mind open to the possibility that your opinions, beliefs, biases, and assumptions might not be accurate, or might no longer be a reflection of reality. You don't have to accept or agree with new or alternative ideas, but you need to be open to them; you need at least to consider them.

Dealing with the persistent false beliefs of others can be a frustrating, exasperating experience. With your own persistence of belief, at least you're in control. You can consciously look at other ideas, and be open to them, or if not open, at least try to understand them so that you can understand the people who believe in them. You may never be able to shift other people from their false, but deeply and sincerely held beliefs. Even with irrefutable evidence, seen by the believer's own eyes, it is common for people to cling to a false belief.

If you are to maximize your effectiveness, you must be ready to abandon cherished or strongly held beliefs when credible evidence shows those beliefs to be in error. And you must be more discerning so that you adopt reality-based beliefs in the first place.

Whenever one of your strongly held beliefs is challenged, pause (if you have time) to use the two-question technique to look at the reality of your belief with fresh eyes and to open up to other possibilities. If you have no time in the moment, take a few moments later to review the situation and apply the two questions. You'll either confirm your belief, or you won't, but either way you'll have a deeper understanding of the situation, and your Reality B will be a better representation of Reality A.

Generalization and Simplification

Generalizations and simplifications, such as anecdotal thinking, stereotyping, demographics, statistics, and simplification of complex subjects are all useful ways of thinking and they are sometimes the only way we can understand a situation. But be alert. You need stay aware that generalization and simplification can strip the reality out of some situations.

Anecdotes and Anecdotal Evidence

An anecdote is a brief story, true or fictional, that makes a point. Anecdotal evidence is the use of a single incident, or a small number of incidents, as proof of a broader truth. Anecdotes and anecdotal evidence are useless for analysis and drawing general conclusions, but they're excellent for communicating in a way that captures the audience's attention.

Anecdotes can distort your thinking if you generalize from them. An anecdote represents a single incident, and is representative of that incident only. That's why anecdotal evidence is so flawed; it represents one or a small number of incidents, not a general truth. Here's a tasteless and extreme (but true) illustration:

In the year 2005, a human finger was found in a salad at a Wendy's fast food restaurant. It was a one-time incident. In all of Wendy's thousands of restaurants, and indeed in all of the more than one hundred thousand fast food restaurants of all kinds, this had never happened before. Because it was such a lurid event, the news media publicized it repeatedly over a period of weeks, and the public was repelled by the thought of a severed human finger in a salad.

The odds of any one customer of Wendy's finding something this repulsive in his or her food was on the order of a billion to one, much less of a chance than winning the lottery. Yet, based on this single piece of anecdotal "evidence" many thousands of customers, who otherwise like Wendy's restaurants and food, stayed away.

In this case, the "anecdote" carried a high emotional charge – disgust, revulsion, and maybe a bit of fear. People didn't think about the reality of the situation and the very low odds of having such an experience. People reacted emotionally to the event, and associated a sense of disgust with Wendy's. You may remember that the finger incident was a fraudulent attempt to extort money from Wendy's by way of the courts, and, in fact, no one had ever actually suffered such an incident. Yet Wendy's business suffered for a time, and may not ever have fully recovered.

If you know what the reality of a situation is, anecdotes can be an excellent way to communicate it; anecdotes are simple stories that can personalize, and add energy and emotion to your communications. I use them frequently in this book to illustrate key points. My anecdotes don't "prove" anything, but, because each of them actually does represent a general truth, they serve as a good way to make the broader, underlying points, which have proven to be true based on other, valid, sources.

An unethical, but legal use of anecdotes is to present one or a few true cases, saying or implying that those cases represent a general truth, when in fact they don't. For instance, a recent advertisement for a weight-loss supplement said something like, "Mary Sue Ralston, of Avoirdupois, Louisiana lost 67 pounds on the Schlimm diet." No doubt Mary Sue truly did lose that weight on that diet, but the commercial didn't say that she also cut down on the amount of food she ate and stuck to a regular plan of exercise. It also didn't say what percentage of people who tried the Schlimm diet were successful in losing weight and keeping it off. Mary Sue's experience was true for her, but it didn't necessarily reflect a general truth.

Another commercial for a well-known brand of pickup truck stated that, "Sam Peck of Bighat, Texas, has been driving his [brand] truck for 250,000 miles, and expects another 100,000." The implication is that your experience with [brand] trucks will be the same as Sam Peck's, even though the actual statistics on truck mileage aren't mentioned. Again, Sam's experience, even if true, doesn't necessarily reflect a broader truth.

The key points: Don't accept anecdotal evidence as representative of a broader reality unless you know the broader reality actually is true. Anecdotes are only representative of the events they describe. Also, anecdotes can be a great way to add emotion and persuasive power to your communications, but remember that it's unethical to assert that the anecdote represents the general reality if in fact it doesn't.

Stereotypes

Stereotyping occurs when we assume individuals have all of the characteristics we associate with a group of similar people, but often they don't. The danger in stereotyping is that you might attribute the perceived common behavior of a class of people to an individual who fits that class, and thus do injustice to the individual. Do you know any people of Irish descent? Are they alcoholics? Do you know any Muslims? Are they terrorists? Are all MBA graduates outstanding managers? Are all senior citizens forgetful? Are all teenagers poor drivers? Do all redheads have hot tempers? Are all Scots thrifty? Are all homeless people lazy? Are all mothers-in-law obnoxious? Are all Chinese-Americans great students? Are all fat people jolly?

Of course not.

Individuals are not stereotypes. If we are to deal with them effectively, we must deal with them as they are as individual people, not as we think most of them are. When we deal with individuals, we find that there are sober Irishmen, non-terrorist Muslims, MBAs who mismanage, senior citizens who don't forget anything, expert teenaged drivers, calm redheads, spendthrift Scots, industrious homeless people, loveable mothers-in-law, stupid Chinese-Americans, and ill-tempered fat men.

Stereotypes are useful. They give us hints about what we *might* find in people, and they help us set up our businesses to serve large populations of customers, but each individual, and each customer, is his/her own person, and should be dealt with individually. Look for the stereotype in each person if you want to, but be prepared to see something else, and to deal with each person based on his or her specific characteristics. Find out what's *real* about each individual, and *never* make assumptions about individuals based on stereotypes.

While I was writing this book, the first two women in history graduated from the US Army's rigorous Ranger School. I paid close attention because I myself graduated from Ranger School many years ago. The event was controversial, and caused a lot of discussion in the news media, and stereotyping was at the heart of it. I heard comments such as (paraphrasing): women don't belong in combat roles because they are a danger to themselves and those around them, women don't have the physical strength to overcome the demands of Rangers in combat; women aren't temperamentally suited for Ranger duty and combat, and on and on. Those opinions may be true for many, even most, women. But at least these two women proved that the stereotype wasn't true for them. Fortunately, in my opinion, (yours may differ) the Army decided to allow people into Ranger School based on their qualifications, not their stereotype. The news reported that 20 women entered that Ranger class, and only two graduated. So the stereotype held mostly true, but wouldn't it have been an injustice for the Army to deny all women access to Ranger School, even if they were qualified for it? Ditto police work, ditto firefighting. and at one time, ditto the right to vote.

Demographics and Statistics

You can survey and demographically define the average American, but you probably can't find a single person who exactly fits the statistical profile of an "average American." If the average American is five feet seven inches tall, weighs 173 pounds, is 42 years old, earns $52,300 per year, and is married with 1.5 children, that's useful information (I made those numbers up, so don't take them as gospel), but I'll bet you don't know a single person who fits that profile. It might be accurate for the population, yet it describes almost no individual people. Yet, the idea of the average American is a useful idea in a broad, general way. If I ask you to tell me about the average teen-ager, and the average senior citizen, or if I ask you to compare the typical democrat with the typical republican, or doctors compared with glass blowers, you can say some meaningful things about each group, can't you? That's the value of demographics and statistics. Even when you don't use numbers to describe them, you have some ideas (stereotypes) about them, and those ideas help you understand the world we live in, don't they? They make a hugely complex world more understandable.

But watch out. Demographics, even when they consist of general impressions rather than statistical analyses, are a form of stereotyping when you apply them to individuals. Individuals almost always differ in important ways from the stereotypes or statistical models that describe them.

Yes, believe it or not, demographic studies – and the statistics that underlie them – are a form of stereotyping, and a very useful form, indeed. We conduct studies in which we ask individual people questions about themselves and their behavior, and we use statistical formulas to draw conclusions about these groups.

By the way, have you noticed that the responses that people make to survey questionnaires are anecdotes? And as such they're only true for the individuals. Yet, when we collect large numbers of them, they become statistics. When do anecdotes become statistics? When the numbers are large enough that we can conclude that they are representative of the larger group. The only difference between anecdotal evidence and statistical evidence is the number of observations. Is one anecdote (or questionnaire in a survey) representative of a population?

No. How about two? Still no. How about ten? Well, maybe. It depends on the size of the population. How about a hundred? Again, it depends on the size of the population of the group. There's a lot of gray area, isn't there? That's what the science (and science it truly is) of statistics deals with. Statistics doesn't do away with gray areas; it helps us understand them.

We can draw a lot of very useful conclusions based on demographics and statistics. We use those conclusions to make important decisions about marketing strategies, political campaigns, product designs, medical treatments, social theories, government laws and regulations, crime fighting tactics, financial policies, tax rates, college admissions, and any number of other ways of dealing with groups of people. It's useful and appropriate to use demographics and statistics to deal with groups of people and institutions, because that's really the only way to understand them as groups. Without demographics and the statistics that underlie them, understanding large groups of people and complex systems would be darn near impossible.

Yet that large truth breaks down when dealing with individuals and very small groups. You can never draw valid conclusions about individuals by assuming that statistics (including demographics, and non-numerical generalizations like stereotypes) are true of them. You'll only be right occasionally and by accident, and you'll be wrong a whole lot more often than you'll be right. If your Reality B about an individual person is based on statistics or stereotypes, your Reality B will often be wrong, or at best only partly right. When you're dealing with individuals – whether you're a salesperson, police officer, medical doctor, or just you and me – you absolutely *must* understand them individually, and deal with them as the specific individuals they are, and not as stereotypes and generalities. If you don't, you're deliberately divorcing yourself from reality, and that leads to injustice and stupid decisions.

Have you ever telephoned or emailed a large business or government agency? Not likely. You were probably treated as if you were the "average customer" with a predetermined set of needs, rather than the individual you are. You probably had to thread your way through a bunch of screening questions designed to categorize you into one of the predetermined problem solutions that research indicates are needed for the target market. You may or may not have ever reached an actual human being, and if you did, that human being was trained (programmed) to treat you the way the research says the average customer should be treated, including extremely polite (but artificial) treatment, and a chipper demeanor that probably seemed rehearsed rather than authentic. You were probably treated to standard responses to the questions you were expected to ask (because those are the questions the "average customer" would ask). And if your questions or problems weren't exactly as the person or system was programmed to deal with, you were met with confusion. Maybe the system finally solved your problem or answered your question (after it made you jump through a lot of hoops, and frustrated you). If it didn't (and if you were lucky) you were passed on to someone who had the authority to deal with you as an individual. Or maybe you simply gave up in frustration.

In business, when you assume that individual customers are the same as the demographic profile of all of your customers, that's when you get into trouble. As you already know, too many businesses, especially large ones whose managers are far removed from customers, train their employees to deal with the target customer, and in doing so condition their employees' unconscious minds with the impression that when they're dealing with you, they're dealing with a target customer (a stereotype), not an individual human being.

That's the danger of demographics and statistics; they tend to condition you, mostly unconsciously, to see individual people as demographics and statistics, rather than the individuals they truly are. Yes, the demographics and statistics help you manage a business efficiently, and profitably, but if you're not careful, those same demographics and statistics bias you to see your individual customers in ways that aren't realistic, in ways that alienate them, and in ways that deny them the service that will keep them coming back to you.

K.I.S.S. (Keep It Simple Stupid)

One of the most time-honored guidelines we have for efficiency is K.I.S.S. – keep it simple, stupid. And it works great, except when it doesn't, and then you can go all kinds of wrong.

Believe it or not, simplicity itself is a complex subject.

First of all, your mind, consciously and unconsciously, craves simplicity. Brain scans and carefully controlled experiments repeatedly show that the mind understands simple ideas more readily than complex ones. No surprise there, but the mind also more readily accepts simple ideas as true, even when they're not true. We accept simple explanations for complex phenomena because, unconsciously, simplicity *feels* better; it feels *true*. Your intuition tells you that simple is true, even when it's not. Simple ideas aren't hard to understand. They require less mental focus, and less memory. They generate fewer negative emotions such as anxiety and frustration, and more positive emotions such as satisfaction and that comfy "aha" sensation we get when we think we understand something important. Your mind likes that, prefers that, and believes that. A false "aha" feels just as good as a true "aha" to the unconscious mind.

So we're geared to accept and to believe the simple version of things; we're wired for simplicity.

Problem: the world is often a complex place; more often than not, in fact. Reality A is often complex, and when we believe a Reality B that's simple, when it's really not, we're getting it wrong, even though it feels so right. Myth #4, which I described in an earlier chapter (we want our businesses to be simple, easy, quick, and cheap), is an expression of this all-to-human desire for simplicity.

My point is not that we shouldn't make decisions when we lack complete understanding of the consequences. We can't always understand the consequences, and the more complex the situation, the less we understand the outcomes of our decisions. My point is that we need to be aware of our desire, our *need*, to simplify, to know when we're doing it, and to *stop* doing it. When we recognize the complexity of a situation, or its simplicity if it is indeed simple, we can make decisions with a full sense of the certainty or uncertainty of the outcome. We can stop creating false expectations, and allow for "I don't know." We can eliminate many of our biases because we're more open to all possible outcomes, rather than seeing a narrow range of outcomes based on false or distorted expectations. We can become more open to seeing the situation as it unfolds and adjusting to it, rather than insisting that everything is okay until failure smacks us in the face.

It's not easy to resist our need for simplicity because it exposes us to uncertainty, and, as much as the mind craves simplicity, it rejects uncertainty. In fact, as you'll see later in the section on coherence and pattern recognition, the mind's coherence function creates a sense of certainty, even when it's false certainty. So your conscious mind needs to overcome two innate urges: it needs to learn to reject the urge to simplify when the situation is complex, and it needs to reject the urge for certainty when your Reality B is anything but certain.

Cause and Effect

When things coincide in time or location, our unconscious impulse is to assume cause and effect. We rarely pause to call on our conscious thinking to determine whether it actually is cause and effect, merely coincidence, or that we simply don't know one way or the other.

Consider this familiar scenario:

I caught a cold on an airplane yesterday. Today, I have a cold, and yesterday I was breathing all that stale air from the other passengers, so of course that's where I caught the cold.

Really? Or was it merely a coincidence, and there was actually no connection between your cold and the airplane ride? Is there any way to know for sure? No. But the mind saw a connection, probably fueled by some beliefs about catching colds, and it concocted the story about catching cold on an airplane. It may or may not be true. We just don't know.

In a community north of San Francisco, there's a controversy involving inoculations; injections of medicine intended to make children immune to certain diseases, such as whooping cough, or polio, or others. A lot of families in that area believe that inoculations can cause autism in children because, in fact, some children actually were diagnosed with autism after being inoculated. These concerned parents assume cause and effect – inoculations increase the risk of autism – and won't allow their children to be inoculated. The concerned parents understand that this puts their children at risk for whooping cough or other diseases, but they believe that autism represents a far greater risk, so, no inoculation for their kids.

It all sounds pretty reasonable, doesn't it?

But there's another side, which insists that inoculations have nothing to do with autism. They believe that autism developed in some kids simply as a result of the normal occurrence of autism in a population. There are bound to be some kids who got inoculated and also developed autism, but one had nothing to do with the other.

Who's right? Does inoculation cause autism? Or doesn't it? Should the kids be inoculated or not?

I don't know how this controversy will ultimately play out, but I do know that it was caused by flawed habits of mind, principally the ones that make us notice a correlation, jump to either the cause and effect conclusion or the coincidence conclusion. Then, having jumped to that conclusion, they cling to it as if it were fact. The flaw in the thinking of both sides was the lack of "I don't know" and the insistence on "I do know" even when that wasn't justified.

"I know" is a closed position, not open to new evidence, other points of view, or a wider range of possibilities, and it generates false certainty. "I don't know" on the other hand, is a position that encourages a search for new information and better understanding. It's open to other points of view, and a wide range of possibilities. And, most importantly, "I don't know" doesn't lock you into a rigid conclusion, partial understanding, or a limited range of possibilities.

The two-question technique puts you into a state of "I don't know" (even when you think you *do* know) because it asks you to think about other possibilities and to search for more information about a subject.

The awareness you need to cultivate is that there are three, not two, alternatives to consider: cause and effect, coincidence, or "I don't know." The new habit of mind you need to cultivate is this: Whenever there is doubt (even minor doubt), controversy (both sides can't be right), or any of those nagging head, heart, or gut signals alerting you that something is "off," you need, consciously, to adopt the "I don't know" position. That'll keep you open to more information, a wider range of possibilities, and the willingness to take into account other points of view, and it'll make you a better decision-maker.

Either/Or

Let me start this section with a couple of quotes from the book, *Born to Believe*, by Andrew Newberg, MD and Mark Waldman:

The brain has a tendency to reduce everything to as few components as possible. In the hidden recesses of the inferior parietal lobe, there exists a cognitive function that puts abstract concepts into polarized dyads, or dualistic terms. ... It is easier for the brain to first quantify objects into pairs, and then to differentiate them into opposing groups: light or dark, happy or sad, fact or fiction, good or evil, right or wrong, Republican or Democrat, and so on. ... Furthermore, once an oppositional dyad is created, the brain will then impose an emotional bias on each part of the dyad. Thus, once we divide objects, people, and ideals into groups, we will tend to express a preference for one and a dislike for the other.

When individuals are randomly placed into different groups, they feel stronger about their own group and tend to feel negatively about other groups ... thus simply being a part of a group results in ill will toward other groups." This inborn 'us-versus-them' mentality can be easily converted into racism [or homophobia, or xenophobia, etc.].

Our minds want to simplify things into either/or, them/us, good/bad, happy/sad, winning/losing, and so on. It's a form of "dualism." Our minds find it easier to perceive the world in pairs of opposites, so our unconscious minds create perceptions of reality that tend to be dualistic. But the world isn't necessarily a dualistic place. Things don't always, or even often, come in oppositional pairs. It may seem like it to us because our minds want to construct Reality B that way, even when Reality A isn't at all dualistic. Events are rarely purely good or purely bad. Experiences aren't ecstatic or miserable, they come in all shades and degrees of happy, sad, and neutral, and often an unpredictable mix of all of them. Groups that don't include us aren't always bad, wrong, or undesirable, and our group (family, club, gang, school, neighborhood, sports team, political party, race, religion, etc.) isn't always good, right, or desirable.

I was listening to a radio talk show the other day and the host of the show asked the guest, a prominent politician, a question on a complex subject. For our purposes, the question doesn't matter. What matters is that the host insisted that the guest give a yes or no answer to the question. When the guest demurred, politely, wanting to give a more complete answer, the host verbally attacked him, saying something like, "Can't you give a simple yes or no answer? Why do you have to be so evasive? What are you afraid of?"

I found myself, for a moment, seduced by the host, thinking to myself, "Yeah, why is this bozo being so evasive? What's he hiding?" Then I caught myself. I know full well that the human mind tends to reduce things to simplistic dualisms, yet I had fallen into that very trap, at least for a moment, until my conscious mind asserted itself by triggering my awareness of my own tendency toward dualism, even when it's a false dualism.

It's a trap we all fall into unless we sharpen our awareness so that we can alert ourselves when we're doing it, and cultivate the two-question habit in order to bring ourselves out of our distortions and back to reality; Reality A, that is.

WYSIATI (what you see is all there is) and Blind Spots

The unconscious mind operates as if the information it knows is all the information there is. In fact, to the unconscious mind, what it knows *is* all there is to know, and if some of what it knows is erroneous, those errors will be woven into the story it tells the conscious mind. Memories, impressions, facts, and even imagination provide the basis for unconscious ideas and impressions. The mind's coherence function (more on coherence in the next section) weaves it all together, evaluates various possibilities, selects the one that has the greatest coherence, and then delivers its conclusions to the conscious mind, which tends to accept it all as true. Nobel Prize laureate Daniel Kahneman in his book *Thinking, Fast and Slow* calls it "WYSIATI" or what you see is all there is.

The validity of this kind of thinking depends completely on what information the unconscious mind has available or can generate. The unconscious mind doesn't know what it doesn't know; it has no sense of blind spots or the possibility of additional information. It simply takes what it has, makes "sense" of it (creates coherence), and delivers the results to our conscious minds, whether those results reflect reality or not.

WYSIATI rules unconscious thinking unless we're aware of this tendency and use our conscious minds to override our unconscious conclusions and impressions, and to seek more information to add to the thought process.

WYSIATI causes us to jump to conclusions based on limited, often insufficient, evidence. It causes us to have unwarranted confidence in our conclusions. The confidence that individuals have in their beliefs depends mostly on the quality of the story they can tell about what they see, even if they see little. Have you ever noticed that people who only see one-sided evidence are more confident of their judgments than those who see both sides?

WYSIATI leaves blind spots in your knowledge and awareness. But WYSIATI isn't the only source of blind spots. Sometimes, habits such as generalization, limiting beliefs, cause and effect, the either/or assumption, and the other distortions you'll be reading about in this chapter, can create blind spots and false beliefs that are every bit as distorting to your perceptions (your Reality B) as WYSIATI.

It's the consistency (coherence) of the information that matters for a good story, not its completeness. In fact, you'll often find that knowing little makes it easier to fit everything you know into a believable story. The coherence function tends to create such a story, and it suppresses doubt and ambiguity.

It is the job of the conscious mind to be alert for WYSIATI and blind spots in order to seek, or at least allow for the possibility, of other information and other impressions. But how (because it all happens unconsciously) can we make our conscious minds aware of our WYSIATI and blind spots?

The solution to WYSIATI and blind spots is not to know everything; that's impossible. The solution is to know that you might not know everything you need to know, and when the situation is important, to use the two-question habit to extend your conscious and unconscious thinking to encompass what can reasonably be learned in a reasonable time. Be aware that your mind wants to manufacture certainty from incomplete and uncertain information, so that you can be open to a wider range of possibilities, and reduce the information gaps and blind spots. The aim is to be as responsible as you possibly can for reaching rational, fully-informed (or as fully-informed as possible) conclusions, perceiving the most accurate possible Reality B, and taking responsible actions and generating realistic expectations (sometimes including no expectations at all by taking the highly adaptable stance of "I don't know").

Coherence and Pattern Recognition

There's a lot of brain/mind science revealing that our minds are "coherence machines" given to making sense of our world and revealing patterns to us, whether or not our perceptions are accurate or the patterns we perceive actually exist. Usually they do, sometimes they don't. The mind's coherence function, which includes our talent for pattern recognition, is an indispensible ability and we couldn't survive without it, but as you have seen in this book for other habits of mind, it can sometimes lead us seriously astray.

In my home, we have a beautiful painting of a forested mountain, seen from a couple miles distance. On the mountain are two side-by-side rock formations about two-thirds up the mountainside. Beneath the rock formations is another rock formation. My mind can't help seeing these formations and their shadows as a face on the mountainside. It's not a face, of course, merely rocky shapes and shadows. But my mind's pattern recognition insists on interpreting the configuration on the mountain as the face of a gruff old man. My conscious mind knows better, but my unconscious mind can't help seeing the "face" and sensing how wrong, how "off" it is. Mountains don't have faces (except for Mt. Rushmore) so I don't really believe it's a face, yet the face-like pattern disturbs my perceptions and ruins, for me, what would otherwise be a beautiful artwork.

I'm not the only one whose unconscious mind does this. Some years ago the world was treated to photographs of the surface of the planet Mars. For a few days, the newspaper headlines were filled with reports of a human (or near human) face on the planet's surface, along with abundant speculation about how such a likeness came to be in a spot where no human, or any life other than microbes, had ever existed. You can imagine what speculations fertile minds came up with. In fact, it would be a surprise, given the size of the planet and the millions (billions?) of instances of rocks, drifting sand, and shadows, if there were no configurations that resembled two paired features (eyes?), a nearby vertically oriented feature (nose?), and another nearby horizontal feature (mouth?) within a crater or upon a mound or other roundish feature (head?).

The face on the mountain and the face on Mars were not imaginary, they were real. But they weren't faces. Our Reality B perceived them as faces, but the Reality A about them is that they were nothing more than randomly occurring rocks, sand, and shadows, that our minds' coherence function – specifically the pattern recognition aspect of the coherence function – convinced us had meaning and recognizable shapes.

My unconscious mind is both an artist and a storyteller, and so is yours. Our minds take what we see and remember, and build coherent stories to explain it. We believe these stories because our unconscious minds attach emotional meaning to them and make sure they seem reasonable to us. We're built that way, and in the normal course of events, in a familiar world, our perceptions, and the stories our unconscious minds tell us about them, give us a pretty good sense of the Reality A of our world.

But sometimes our unconscious minds get it wrong. Our WYSIATI – the "what you see is all there is" in our heads – is often incomplete or erroneous. Our mental models are sometimes skewed. Our dozen distortions sometimes twist our perceptions from reality to something else, and as a result our Reality B sometimes doesn't match Reality A. Our unconscious minds are working fine. All the connections connect as they should, and we're sane and reasonable. But the raw materials of knowledge and mental models, plus our various built-in biases, are incomplete or flawed, so our unconscious minds (our coherence machines) get it wrong through no deficiency in our wiring, but through flawed and incomplete information and beliefs. It's the human equivalent of GIGO in computers – garbage-in-garbage-out – or in human terms, incomplete or erroneous information in, flawed Reality B out.

This coherence function of ours is really quite amazing and it's an extremely valuable ability. It allows us (usually) to jump to well-founded conclusions that are reasonable and keep us grounded in a Reality B that's well-matched with Reality A. But sometimes the coherence function gets it wrong. If the situation isn't important, then no harm, no foul, but when it's important, we've got to get it right because the consequences of wrong decisions can be devastating to our businesses and our lives.

Here's the key question: If our coherence functions feed us convincing stories that seem to right to us, and they do it unconsciously, how can we know when they're in error, and what can we do about it?

You'll never know if the conclusions that make up your Reality B are in error unless you consciously examine them and seek more information to confirm or refute them. But life is full of experiences and activities, and who has the time or the willingness to re-examine every experience, every belief, and every impression our minds come up with? Nobody, that's who, yet we still need, especially for matters that are important to our businesses and our lives, to make sure our Reality B is sound and our decisions wise. The problem is to identify which conclusions supplied by our unconscious minds might be wrong, and then either verify them or reshape them into something more accurate.

To do that, we need to learn from brain/mind science to see which stories that our minds provide us are most likely to be wrong and to put our attention on those. There are four situations you can use to alert yourself when to use the two-question technique to put your conscious mind in charge so that it can verify or improve your ideas and to feed your unconscious mind more information so it can do a better job of thinking for you.

Complexity: As we saw earlier, both your conscious and unconscious minds prefer simple ideas. They generate simplicity, even when the reality of the situation is complex, and they find simplicity more believable, even when it's false. So, when confronted by complexity, or when simplicity doesn't feel quite right, and when the situation is important, you should consciously initiate the two-question technique to verify your thinking, or to reach more thoughtful conclusions, and therefore a more accurate Reality B.

Uncertainty: Also, as we saw earlier, your conscious and unconscious thinking prefer certainty; they want "I know" not "I don't know." So, when the situation and/or its outcome are uncertain, and especially when you know things are uncertain, but you still feel a sense of certainty about your actions and conclusions, you need to double-check your sense of certainty by consciously engaging the two-question technique.

Novelty/Unfamiliarity: Your unconscious mind has learned over the course of your life how to deal with routine, familiar situations, and it does so with remarkable reliability and ease. When you are confronted by surprises and unfamiliar situations, however, your mind tries to relate the experience to something familiar in your past, and to deal with the current situation as if it were similar. So, when confronted by surprises and novelty, even when you feel comfortable with your reactions and thoughts, and again, when the situation is important and you can't afford to be wrong, you need to engage the two-question technique.

"Off" signals: Your unconscious mind is always at work, and when you encounter situations that conflict with your experience, with what you think you know, with your mental models, or when things simply don't make sense, your unconscious mind sends you signals – emotional responses, "gut feelings," and intuitions – that something isn't right. It's that "off" feeling (different for everyone) that you so often don't notice or ignore because it doesn't seem important. Well, when the situation is important, you need to pay attention to the "off" feeling, whatever form it takes for you, and look more deeply into the situation. Even when feelings of "off-ness" are subtle and easy to ignore, but the consequences are important, you need to engage the two-question technique.

The coherence function of your unconscious mind works, and it works extremely well. You just have to feed it good information so that it can feed you good conclusions.

Expectations, Selective Perception, and the Confirmation Bias

Expectations

An expectation is an idea of the future that you consciously or unconsciously believe will happen. If your expectations are based on a clear sense of reality (an accurate Reality B) and an understanding that the future is uncertain, and if you're open to the negative and positive possibilities, you'll be able to adjust to unexpected situations without much internal distress. You'll be able to deal with the situation effectively.

Problems occur when your expectations aren't based in reality and/or when you get locked into them.

When your expectations are based on a distorted perception of reality and something goes wrong, you're surprised. Your (flawed) sense of reality leads you to think, "This shouldn't be happening. It doesn't make sense," and you thrash around trying to fix the situation or revise your expectations, still grounded in a false perception of reality, a flawed Reality B. One of three things happens: (1) you continue to thrash around with growing frustration and diminishing effectiveness, (2) you make decisions that, by chance, lead to the desired result (not very likely), or (3) you come to the realization that you need to understand the situation better, take steps to do so, and revise your expectations based on a better understanding, a better Reality B. Of course, #3 is what you should have done in the first place.

What happens when you get "locked in" to unrealistic expectations? You're rigidly committed to making the expectation happen despite the problems, interruptions, and frustrations that "mysteriously" crop up. It doesn't occur to you to challenge your understanding of reality, so you push to achieve the expectations that seem right and realistic. You think it's simply a matter of determination and commitment, so you push and push, all the while puzzled by the inability to get the job done the way it "should" be done.

The only way out of this dilemma of unrealistic expectations, is to develop the awareness that your perception of what's real may be flawed, and at the same time to develop the ability to be open to other possibilities. That leads to better understanding of reality, which leads to more realistic expectations.

So, when the stakes are important you need to get your expectations right, or at least acknowledge that they're uncertain so that you'll be mentally prepared to adjust and adapt to the emerging situation. The two-question technique will set you on the right path.

Selective Perception

Selective perception is an interesting variant of expectations. Selective perceptions occur when you have expectations about people, events, information, or anything else. If you believe, for instance, that the leader of your country is wise and capable, you will tend to perceive everything he does as right and proper. If you believe he is stupid and incompetent, you will tend to perceive everything he does as bungling and ineffective. In other words, you'll notice what he does that meets your expectations, and not notice, or rationalize, what doesn't match up with your expectations. If, on the other hand, you maintain an open, receptive state of mind about him, you will make objective, realistic assessments of each of his various decisions and actions and you will have a more realistic sense of his presidency.

People see and understand what they expect to see and understand much more easily than they absorb something that doesn't fit with their established ideas or expectations about the world. When you have an expectation, your interpretation of events will tend to reinforce the expectation. If you have a particular belief, even if it's a false belief, you will tend to observe the world in ways that are consistent with that belief. If you have a bias, you tend to see things that support your bias. Your mind "selects" what it prefers and "selectively" interprets it to conform to your desires and preferences.

There's an interesting, and all too common flip side to this coin. When people selectively give out information, they're distorting reality, sometimes deliberately and sometimes unconsciously. When politicians do it we call it "spin." When marketing people do it, we call it advertising. When you and I do it, we're either called liars, or if we're unconscious about it, we're called everything from mistaken to stupid.

When you selectively perceive information and events, you are denying yourself a full understanding of reality. Your resulting decisions and behavior will be flawed, and your effectiveness will be diminished.

First impressions are considered important because they start to create positive, or negative, selective perceptions. When you meet someone for the first time, if he has a sweaty handshake and won't make eye contact, doesn't that make a poor first impression, and doesn't that affect the way you perceive him from that point on? It's much easier to make a first impression, good or bad, on someone than it is to reverse an impression after it has been made.

Put it in a business context. The whole purpose of product branding is to create selective perceptions in your target markets. If you can convince your potential customers that your product is best, they will selectively perceive it that way. A strong brand makes the entire sales process easier because people will tend to hear the positive about the product and discount the negative. The same is true after the purchase; customers will tend to see the positive in their purchases. The opposite is also true; negative expectations lead to negative perceptions.

The point, of course, is to be aware of the human tendency toward selective perceptions and to develop the ability to see through your own selectivity so that you can have a more accurate perception of reality.

The Confirmation Bias

You've probably heard the term "confirmation bias" and know it means that we pay attention to and interpret information in ways that tend to confirm our existing beliefs. That's only partly right. Confirmation bias works much more unconsciously and insidiously than that.

Daniel Kahneman, the Nobel Laureate I quote often in this book, explains it like this (paraphrased):

Confirmation bias is an innate operation of your unconscious mind. When presented with an idea – a hypothesis – your unconscious mind tests the hypothesis by looking for confirming evidence. It has a positive bias. It tries to believe the hypothesis rather than refute it or take an objective stance. Your unconscious mind is gullible and biased to believe; your conscious mind is in charge of doubting and unbelieving, but it's sometimes focused on other things or has no information that would stimulate disbelief. Notice especially the sentence, "Your unconscious mind is gullible and biased to believe; your conscious mind is in charge of doubting and unbelieving."

The conclusion: People notice and believe data that are likely to be compatible with the beliefs they currently hold, and interpret data in ways that tend to confirm those beliefs. They ignore, rationalize, or simply don't notice data that conflict with their beliefs.

Kahneman also noted that the confirmatory bias of your unconscious mind favors uncritical acceptance of exaggerations of the likelihood of extreme and improbable events. Look for instance (my example, not his) at one of modern history's most horrific events and the exaggerated impact it has had on our lives since September 11, 2001. The terrorist attacks on US soil and airspace on that date killed roughly 4,000 people (about 0.001% of the population of the USA). Cancer, heart disease, automobile accidents, crime, or a hundred other causes kill far more people. The risk of dying of any of these causes is enormously greater than the risk of dying by terrorist attack. But they're routine, normal, unremarkable. That's Reality A.

But the scene on 9/11 was horrific, and we all saw it on television and in print, continuously, for weeks. We consciously and unconsciously engraved the horror of it deeply and ineradicably in our minds and memories, and we can still easily evoke the emotions that it stimulated in us. In the years since then, our perceptions about terrorists, and by association Muslims, have solidified, and our national policies, and many would say our very national character, have shifted significantly toward security at the expense of liberty (debatable, but you can make the case). 9/11 was both extreme and improbable, and it did exactly as Kahneman describes – it engraved itself in our conscious and unconscious minds in extreme ways, coloring our lives as has no other event in our lifetimes. That's Reality B for most of us.

Your conscious mind has the power to intercede and override your unconscious expectations, selective perceptions, and confirmation bias, but it doesn't do so unless, and this is critical, you are alerted to these effects and consciously override them.

The two-question technique gives you the tool you need to put them in their proper perspective.

Emotions

What do you do when someone gets angry with you, gets in your face, or makes threats? Do you get angry in response? Do you withdraw to avoid the anger and your own emotional reaction? Do you "numb out" in confusion? Or do you allow yourself to feel however you feel (angry, fearful, confused) but force yourself to listen to the message within the anger, and behave appropriately to the situation rather than in response to the anger?

The latter response is the most effective of course, but it's not the one that comes naturally to most of us.

Most people react emotionally to emotion directed at them; usually that's a mistake. Emotions distort your sense of what's real. The stronger the emotion, the greater the distortion. If you're responding emotionally then you're distorting a reality that was already distorted by the person directing emotions toward you; a double dose of distortion. Malcolm Gladwell makes the point in his best-selling book, *Blink*:

> *Have you ever tried to have a discussion with an angry or frightened human being? You can't do it. You might as well try to argue with your dog.*

> *[Emotional] Arousal leaves us mind-blind. Most of us, under pressure, get too aroused, and past a certain point, our bodies begin to shutting down so many sources of information that we start to become useless.*

Why are emotions important? Because they're motivators. They're signals of importance. They can add a sense of reality to your mental models, even when those models aren't actually realistic. And they can be signals for you to take a closer look at your Reality B. Let me say more about each of these points.

Emotions are motivators, and they can be extremely strong motivators. We've all seen people in a rage, doing unthinkable things that they'd never do in less emotional circumstances. We've all seen people in love, doing things that don't otherwise make sense. We go to great lengths to relieve and avoid strong negative emotions like fear, anger, and grief, and to stimulate and hold on to the strong positive emotions, like joy, peace, love, and deep satisfaction. The problem is that when in an emotional state, positive or negative, we tend to "go unconscious" unless we insert our awareness into the situation and put our conscious minds in charge.

Emotions are signals of importance. We don't get emotional about trivialities, yet we get very emotional about things of importance. And by "importance" I mean what's important to our conscious and unconscious minds. We've all seen people go off the deep end about something that seems totally inconsequential to us. But to the person in the emotional state there is importance to the situation, whether we see it or not, whether we agree on its importance or not.

And believe it or not, emotions can add a sense of reality to our mental models, even when they're mainly imaginary. For example, I recently returned from a photographic safari in Africa. At one point our Land Rover vehicle was extremely close to an agitated and nervous bull Cape Buffalo. Let me tell you, a Cape Buffalo can be a very scary beast. Our guide, who knew about buffalo behavior, told us there was no danger, so I was able to calm myself and enjoy the experience. But another member of our party, I'll call him Harry, was clearly in a state of fear, imagining all the devastating things an enraged Cape Buffalo could do to our Land Rover and us. Harry knew beyond a doubt – he absolutely KNEW – that it was going to attack us momentarily. Scientists have learned that strong emotions lend a sense of reality to our thoughts, even when they are not based on actual reality. Harry's fear lent his thoughts of devastation from a buffalo attack a sense of reality, so much so, that he couldn't accept our guide's assurances, and was absolutely convinced of the impending disaster. Later, Harry's anger persisted, and even though nothing bad had happened, he accused our guide of endangering us, and even wrote a letter to the safari management to complain. Fear made his mental model both "real" and unshakeable. I can cite other examples in which grief, anger, and even joy and hope add false "reality" to our mental models. There's a lot of good science attesting to this effect; you'll have to take my word for it, or read up on it yourself.

Finally, emotions can be an indicator to our conscious minds that something might be out of whack with Reality B. We get upset when things don't turn out the way we want them to, or when people challenge what we "know" to be true. "Upset" means emotional, angry, anxious, disappointed, irritated, and even surprised and amazed. Our expectations and our beliefs are based on our view of the world; Reality B. When something or someone violates our sense of reality, we get upset. That's a signal. Either the something or someone that upset us is wrong, and we're right, or we're wrong, or both. Either way, it's wise to consciously check in and verify our own sense of reality, and to do that, you need to be open to the possibilities, even when some of the possibilities challenge your beliefs. Don't assume that you're idea of reality is right and don't assume that you're wrong; be open to the possibility that either case might turn out to be true.

Here's the key to dealing with emotions, and benefitting from them rather than being overcome by them: First, you need to be aware that the unconscious mind generates emotions, always in response to a situation or thought, and delivers that emotion into the awareness of the conscious mind. You also need to know that you should never suppress or ignore emotions because the very fact that you have them indicates that something of importance (to you) is occurring. But, and this is a HUGE but, you should never unconsciously react to your emotions, at least not your stronger ones. If your boss or spouse is screaming angrily at you and you find your own anger rising, motivating you to scream (or worse) back at them, you need to alert your conscious mind not to suppress or ignore the emotion, but to observe it, and try to understand what's actually happening. What's Reality A? Something really important is motivating your boss or spouse to scream at you. What is it? You need to know. It's a time to be ruled by objectivity, not anger, because if it's so very important to your boss or spouse, it's potentially important to you, and an angry response from you will make the situation worse, much worse. To be sure, when you're being consciously objective, you'll still *feel* angry (or fearful if that's the way you respond to anger from others), but you need your conscious mind to be in charge and objective so that you'll be able to see through your own anger (or fear, or whatever), and understand the situation in order to deal with it effectively.

The very fact that emotions have arisen, in yourself or in someone else, is both a "trigger" that stimulates your thoughts and behavior and an "alert" signaling something you need to notice. Triggers and alerts are important tools. An emotional "alert" is a signal telling you that something important is happening that you need to be consciously aware of, and that your emotional response should "trigger" you to launch into intentional and constructive rather than reactive and destructive behavior. I'll have more to say about triggers and alerts later.

The most concise explanation of how to deal with emotions comes from, of all places, a mystery novel by an obscure author. In *The Long Mile* by Clyde W. Ford, the author states:

> *Express. Repress. Observe. Three ways to handle emotions. It's good to express them, but not always safe. Repress them and they eat you up from inside. You can always observe them, watching what emotions do inside your body. Observe emotions and they pass through you like waves passing through water. Then you can use them as the guides they're meant to be, and not the rulers we let them become.*

The first thing to remember is that emotions never hurt anyone. They're merely feelings that come and go. Even strong emotions always fade away, leaving you with the consequences of your responses. It's our *reactions* to emotions that can lead to problems. Use emotions as "...*the guides they're meant to be.*"

The second thing about emotions is that you can't stop them, and you shouldn't try. You can repress emotions, but that's not really getting rid of them. It's just pretending they're not affecting you and behaving outwardly as if there were no emotion. Psychiatrists tell us that repressing emotions leads to longer term consequences like poor health, prolonged stress, and other unpleasant effects. Be that as it may, our concern is that you learn to deal with emotions in ways that support effectiveness and lead to success. And responding to emotion with emotion doesn't do that.

So you need to learn to pay attention to your emotions as if you were an uninvolved observer. Observe them, and learn how to see and hear what needs to be seen and heard through the emotion, and how to behave effectively while in an emotional state.

You would think positive emotions like excitement, love, and joy would always be good, and negative emotions like fear, hate, anger, grief, and disgust would always be bad. You might not even recognize some emotions for what they are. Apathy, indifference, peace, and contentment, for instance, are low-energy emotional states, but they can exert a powerful influence on your behavior. Any emotion can contribute to or detract from effectiveness and success, depending on the situation and your response to the emotion. It all depends on the situation, your ability to recognize your own emotional state and the emotional states of those around you, and, most importantly, your ability to function effectively while awash in the presence of emotions. The key is to focus on reality rather than letting emotion distort it.

The two-question technique doesn't eliminate your emotions, but it does force you to think rationally, even when flooded by emotion. It helps you focus your attention on the situation, rather than what it feels like, and that gets you back to a mindset that'll help you touch base with Reality A.

Projection and the "Me-Bias"

Projections

We think, usually unconsciously, that the way we experience the world is the way the world actually is, and that others think and perceive it the same way.

Have you ever said, "If I were in your shoes, I would…"? Did you notice that you were actually putting the other person in *your* shoes? You were saying what you would do in the other person's place, in effect, saying what the other person *should* do. That's what projection is all about, but it goes deeper. It's more than "should." It's a special kind of assumption, usually an unconscious one, that the way you view the world is the way the world is, and that the way you think about things is the way everyone thinks about those things.

If you ask anyone if the way he or she thinks about things is the way everyone thinks about them, the conscious-mind answer for most of us would be an automatic, "No. Not everyone thinks like I do." But your unconscious mind doesn't know this. It's another kind of WYSIATI. It knows how you think and what you think, and unless your conscious mind reins it in, it unconsciously, and falsely, "knows" that your way is *the* way that people think. Projections are almost always driven by unconscious "knowledge" about what's true, and of course that truth seems true for all, or at least it does until you consciously examine it and find that there can be other ways of thinking.

I once had a conversation with a woman in which the subject of racial differences came up. Something she said (I can't remember her exact words) made me think to myself, "What!? Can she possibly believe that?" So I asked her, "Do you believe that all blacks [this was before "African American" became the accepted terminology] would change to white if they could do so merely by snapping their fingers?" Her entirely sincere answer was, "Yes, of course." There was no doubt, no second thought, no wondering. There was just simple certainty. To her, that's just the way it was. If I had tried to talk her into a different point of view, she would have been puzzled at why I was trying to deny the truth; not the truth "as she saw it," but the plain, obvious-to-everyone truth. In those days, I didn't know what it was called but it was my first lesson in projection.

Here's a less extreme (but more relevant to entrepreneurship) example of two projections that we often find in business.

Patricia was the owner of a small business in Northern California. She was praised by all who knew her for her ability to get results. Her friends say she's the hardest working person they know. No matter what it takes, Pat gets the job done.

Sal was the general manager of Patricia's landscape supply business. Sal was a hard working guy, too, and Patricia and Sal saw eye-to-eye on almost everything. They enjoyed a cooperative working relationship, and Patricia almost never had to "be the boss."

One day, when Sal balked at Patricia's idea of creating an Emergency Room for Plants, they had the following conversation:

Sal: I'll do anything you want, of course, after all, it *is* your business, but this doesn't make any sense to me. It's just not worth the effort and work of creating a Plant Emergency Room, staffing it, and publicizing it.

Patricia: But it will make us unique in our market. Effort and work don't matter. What matters is the result.

Sal: I like the result, too, but the work and hassle don't justify the result. We're already overworked and flooded with details that don't contribute much to the business. This will just make it worse.

Patricia: I don't know how to say it any more clearly. The result is the only thing that matters. The work, the details, the hassle are just what you have to do to get the job done. Sometimes, in order to get the results you want, you just have to suck it up and push through the work.

Sal: It just occurred to me that you and I see the world differently when it comes to the balance of work and results. I've always had a sense that the amount of work done should be in some reasonable proportion to the value of the results you're going for. I thought everyone saw it that way, but you don't. You really don't think about, and don't even really care about what it takes to get the result you want, you just decide on the goal (the result) and push for it no matter what it takes. Is that right?

Patricia: Well of course it's right. How could anyone ever get anything done if you worried about how hard it will be or how much work would be needed or how much hassle you'd have to put up with. I thought everyone knew that. It's just so basic, so human!

Sal: To me, it's more basic and more human to balance the goal with what it takes to make it happen. How could anybody think differently? That's just the way it is.

The discussion went on for a while, and fortunately Patricia and Sal each trusted and respected the other enough to listen, and really hear what the other was actually saying. Still, each viewpoint was so deeply and unconsciously ingrained that it was taken as a universal truth. To Patricia, it was a basic reality of the world – work and hassle are irrelevant, you don't even think about them – you do what it takes to get the job done. To Sal, it was a basic reality of the world, you always balance work and hassle against the goal. Sometimes the goal just wasn't worth it. Each of them was *projecting* his/her Reality B on the world and on each other, believing without question that it was the way of things.

That's how projection works. Your conscious and unconscious understanding of the world becomes, to you, the way the world <u>is</u>. You don't experience it as your point of view, but as the fundamental truth of things.

The problem arises, of course, when you behave on the basis of your reality with the unconscious (but false) belief that it's everyone's reality, and expect results consistent with that. And others are doing the same thing toward you. When someone behaves differently from your projection, you take it as a kind of violation of what's right, proper, and effective.

The way to deal with projections is to become aware of yours and alert to the possibility that others may be projecting their views on you. The two-question technique helps you do that.

The Me-Bias

I'm going to quote Kahneman again:

"...neither children nor adults have a well-developed capacity to distinguish the accuracy of their own beliefs. In fact, adults are particularly vulnerable with regard to maintaining self-deceptive beliefs, especially when comparing their own intelligence and attractiveness with other peoples'. For example, in various surveys conducted over the years, approximately 90 percent of the respondents believed that they were smarter, healthier, and more industrious than the average individual.

Most people…overestimate their personal abilities, and unfortunately their inflated beliefs cause them to suspend their ability to test reality. "

We're biased and self-deceptive about ourselves, and by extension those we love and with whom we associate, or feel an affinity. You know it's true of others, don't you? We all know people who exaggerate their own abilities and their own beauty, and who have an inflated sense of their self worth. We don't see it in ourselves, but we readily see it in others. Why, then, isn't it obvious to us that, if others inflate their self-perceptions, we're probably doing it too? Well, if we're inflating our sense of self, doesn't that make us believe that we're a bit more perceptive than all those other people? Don't we see things a bit more clearly than they do? Don't we know ourselves better than they do? And isn't our internal experience of ourselves the truest test of our internal reality? Of course we're the best judges of ourselves. It must be true because it *feels* so true, so certain, and if others weren't so biased toward themselves, they'd see it too.

You can see how this me-bias becomes self-fulfilling and circular in its reasoning.

There's a negative version of the me-bias, in which, because of early conditioning in life, some people come to see themselves as inferior, less worthy, or somehow not as deserving as others. Either way – positive or negative – the me-bias leads you away from the reality of yourself, into self-deception.

Actually, the me-bias can be good thing; probably a survival characteristic of humanity. When we see ourselves so positively, even when others don't, it makes us more willing to take on difficult tasks, assume leadership, and dream ambitious dreams.

Me-bias also extends to our perceptions of those with whom we feel some affiliation, the stronger the affiliation, the stronger the me-bias. It's also a good thing – usually – because it makes us more cohesive and stronger as families, tribes, teams, clubs, races, religions, political parties, cultures, genders, and even whole societies.

But there's a dark side. Me-bias becomes distorted and dysfunctional when it leads to injustice, inappropriate discrimination, perceptions of superiority in ourselves and inferiority in others, and ascribing evil intent to others which isn't based in reality.

I'd venture to say that most of the progress of humanity has its roots in me-bias. I'd also venture to say that most of humanity's man-made tragedies also have their roots in that same me-bias. It's everywhere we look in today's society: black vs white, Muslim vs Christian, Republican vs Democrat, poor vs rich, and on and on.

The lesson for us is that me-bias is another way we distort our perceptions of reality. We don't want to eliminate me/we bias because it's much too useful in our lives. But we do want to understand it and be aware of those times in our lives when it distorts our perceptions and leads us into dysfunctional behavior.

The two-question technique helps put "me" in the right perspective.

Focus Blindness, and Stress

Your unconscious mind has a mind of its own, and it doesn't always see what's there to be seen.

Have you ever been so absorbed with a task or experience that, when someone said something to you, you didn't even hear it? Or maybe you did hear the sound, but had to have it repeated so you could truly hear it? "I'm sorry, I didn't hear what you said, would you please repeat it?"

Have you ever been playing a game, or working so intently, that you injured yourself, yet you didn't feel any pain until later? Soldiers in battle sometimes get wounded, yet feel no pain, and sometimes don't even know they're wounded until later, when they discover, usually with considerable surprise, that they've been wounded. Athletes often get minor injuries without being aware of them until later, when the intensity of the competition abates, and the intensity of the injury becomes noticeable.

When you focus your intention on something, you become less aware of other things, sometimes even blind to them. The more intently you focus, the more blind you become to everything else. And when you're blind, your Reality B won't match up with Reality A.

There is a famous experiment that illustrates the effect. You can see it on the Internet. Go to YouTube and look for "The Monkey Business Illusion." Follow the instructions carefully, and you'll be surprised at your own powers of observation, or lack of them. Don't read the next paragraph until after you've participated on The Monkey Business Illusion.

It's worth the experience. Take a break from reading, and go check out some Monkey Business.

Those of you who watched The Monkey Business Illusion experienced focus blindness in dramatic, if humorous fashion. For those of you who didn't bother to watch, The Monkey Business Illusion consists of six people, three in black shirts and three in white shirts, moving around in a room, passing basketballs back and forth between themselves. Your task, as observer, is to count the number of times people in white shirts pass the ball to other people in white shirts, ignoring the times that people in black shirts pass or receive. It becomes a confusing scene and it requires concentration and focus to get an accurate count. But the point of the exercise isn't to count basketball passes. It's to demonstrate focus blindness. What happens is that, after about thirty seconds of watching, counting, and focusing your attention on the exercise, a person in a gorilla suit walks slowly among the basketball passers, pauses in the middle of the room to beat its chest, and then walks out of the room. Most people don't even notice the gorilla, and they have to watch the video again to convince themselves that there actually was a gorilla and that they missed it completely. Even people like me who think we're savvy, and who know about the Monkey Business Illusion, fall prey to focus blindness. I know about the Monkey Business Illusion, but during the exercise, the color of the background curtain changes, and one of the six people leaves the room and I didn't notice anything but the basketballs and the gorilla. So even though I was prepared to have my powers of observation tested, I was still blind to two significant happenings in the exercise. It's mind-blowing if you don't know about focus blindness.

What happens is that, when confronted with a task that requires focused attention, your mind channels itself to accomplish the task. Your eyes, ears, etc. continue to receive sensory data, but your mind is ignoring everything not related to the task on which you're focused. Your eyes see the gorilla and pass on that visual data, but your mind doesn't pay attention to it because it has nothing to do with the task, counting basketball passes. The resources of the mind are dedicated to accomplishing the task, and it ignores what it considers irrelevant.

Expectations also have something to do with it. If you were told beforehand that a gorilla would appear, you'd have noticed the gorilla, even though you were concentrating on basketball passing. Training and awareness can open your powers of observation so that you're less susceptible to focus blindness, but even the best training can't overcome the mind's need to narrow its perceptions to the task at hand, especially when the task is important and difficult.

Stress is a bit different, but can also diminish your powers of observation. Stress occurs when you're experiencing some form of real or imagined threat – a real danger, the possibility of failure in an important endeavor, a real or imagined embarrassment or possibility of suffering a blow to your self-image; whatever it is that produces stress in you. When stressed, your mind becomes vigilant and poised to deal with the threat. It's a bit like focus blindness in that your mind is looking for something to deal with, to protect you against, or to understand so you can respond in a way that preserves your safety or peace of mind. In other words, your mind is focused in specific ways that cause it to see what it expects to see, or to interpret what it does see in ways that are consistent with whatever is causing the stress.

In either case, whether focus or stress, your mind ignores some perceptions, and/or reshapes some perceptions to be consistent with the (real or imagined) situation. The result is that your mental model (your Reality B) gets distorted, and you're not dealing with reality, but with a flawed perception of reality. And that means decisions and actions that you take when intently focused or stressed may not be completely reality-based.

What's the conclusion? When you're stressed or highly focused, you're not as rational as you think you are. Not completely. The greater the stress, and the more intense the focus, the less rational you are. Yet the mind, especially the unconscious mind (because it automatically seeks and often creates coherency) believes its decisions and actions to be completely rational and justifiable.

In this case the two-question habit doesn't open you up to information and possibilities as much as it awakens you to what's right in front of you. It activates your awareness so that you're more likely to see what's there to be seen, heard, felt, etc.).

Conventional Wisdom and Experts

What's right? What's wrong? Who really knows?

We assume beliefs are true merely because they're widely accepted, and experts are right because they're "experts."

There's nothing wrong with conventional wisdom or with experts and consultants. They're often right, and they got to be "wisdom" and "experts" precisely *because* they're often right. We use them frequently, and we usually get good value from them. But conventional wisdom is the collective beliefs of lots of people, and *because* it's a collection of the beliefs of a lot of individuals, it's subject to the same distortions you're reading about in this chapter. And experts and consultants are the product of conventional education plus their individual experiences, which, again, are subject to these same distortions. When you learn to bypass the distortions, who's to say that your wisdom and your expertise (or at least your judgment) aren't just as good as theirs? Well, as another book asserts, there actually is wisdom in crowds, and there's value in the training, education, and experience of experts, so don't disregard them. They can be valuable, give you important insights, and save you lots of time and money. Just don't abdicate your own judgment in favor of theirs.

Consultants shouldn't make your decisions for you. They can educate you and make recommendations, and if they're effective consultants, they'll make sound recommendations, and you'll often do well to follow them. But keep in mind that consultant's recommendations are based as much on their own experiences, assumptions, beliefs, and biases (their own distortions) as they are on the realities of your situation.

Conventional wisdom shouldn't shape your decisions either, although it can be valuable input, or not. Conventional wisdom is merely the "wisdom" that has stood the test of time or is widely believed. The problem in this case is that a general truth can be, and often is, invalid in a specific situation. Your business is your business, not some average of all businesses. You are you, not some average of all business owners. You're unique. Conventional wisdom doesn't allow for uniqueness. Like stereotyping, it assumes all people and all businesses are alike. So listen to conventional wisdom, learn from it.

And then adapt what you learn to the realities of yourself and your business.

The bottom line about conventional wisdom and experts is this: Make experts explain their findings and justify their recommendations and then think for yourself. Listen to conventional wisdom and then think for yourself. Make up your own mind, and when it's important, test your thinking with the two-question technique.

The Tyranny of Experience

Experience as History: The Way Things Were Isn't Necessarily the Way Things Are

You've probably heard this before: "We've always done it this way and it's always been successful, so we're going to do it this way again." Sooner or later, "We've always done it this way" will become a formula for failure.

Ask K-Mart if "we've always done it this way" is a valid way to manage a business. In 1986, K-Mart was at the top of the heap in its industry, with $36 billion in sales. Management was complacent, and persisted with the same strategy that had been so successful in the past. Meanwhile, WalMart and Target were creating new ways of doing things and siphoning off K-mart's customers. When K-Mart finally woke up, it was too late. In 2004, WalMart was the #1 company on the Fortune 500 list, and the largest retailer in the world. K-Mart was bankrupt and shedding stores in a panic to survive. WalMart changed. K-Mart didn't.

Experience is a great teacher, maybe the greatest. But times and situations change, making old ways of doing things obsolete. And the changes often happen slowly, so the old way of doing things slowly becomes less and less effective as it becomes more and more out of tune with changing reality. Or maybe not. Maybe the tried and true way of doing things is still best.

The point is this: Of course you should learn from experience and respect what has worked for you in the past, but not blindly. You must be open to and willing to adapt to changes. Better yet, you should anticipate changes and take advantage of them rather than being victimized by them. And still better, as an entrepreneur, you should be willing to *initiate* changes that will enable you to achieve your purpose.

Internal Experience: It Makes Life Worth Living, But Sometimes It Lies

I have a very good friend who tells me, when I think she's imagining things, that she trusts her experience, and that her experience *is* her reality. She's both right and wrong, but it took me a lot of years to understand why.

Let's look at Reality A and Reality B from a different point of view, and talk about Reality B as your internal experience. And let's start with something that doesn't carry much emotional load, a rainbow.

Rainbows don't actually exist. They're a creation of our minds in response to physical signals processed by our brains. The factuality of a rainbow is that it's a phenomenon in which electromagnetic waves (light) pass through droplets of water in the atmosphere, with waves of different frequencies being bent at slightly different angles. That's the short version of Reality A; the bent electromagnetic waves are detected by our eyes, and our eyes pass signals into our brains. Our brains interpret these signals as colors. (By the way, colors don't exist in the real world either, but are merely one of the ways our minds make sense of the impulses our eyes send back into our brains.) So, for every rainbow, there's a verifiable factuality out there in the world, and we understand the objective reality of it. But in the internal world of our minds, the experience is a gorgeous arc of colors, suspended in the sky. That's our Reality B, no matter that we can't touch a rainbow. We can't even get near one. As we get closer, it either seems to move farther away or disappears. No one has ever touched a rainbow, or even found the foot of one, where leprechauns supposedly hide their pots of gold.

There's something objectively real in the world that we're perceiving when we experience rainbows. The world creates a phenomenon following the laws of physics and produces objective results in the form of bent rays of light. Our minds perceive that phenomenon and create internal experiences shaped by our senses, our brains' bio-chemical-electrical activity, habits of thinking, habits of being, and mental models. The resulting experience is...a rainbow. Which is true, the objective reality or the internal experience – Reality A or Reality B? They're both true – they both exist, one as objective reality and the other as our internal experience.

And here's the wonderful thing about rainbows; they're beautiful. Do you know anyone who doesn't think so? The beauty of a rainbow lies in our internal experience, not in its factuality. In fact beauty itself exists only within us. The external world is what it is; the perception of beauty (the experience) exists only within us, and it's probably different for each of us.

External reality may trigger our experiences, but it's the internal experience that gives the phenomenon value, stimulates our emotions, and makes us feel alive.

Let's move away from rainbows. What about love? Does love exist in the external world? I say no. Love exists in our internal experiences. To the extent that we can act lovingly and communicate our internal experiences with each other, we can share love, but there's nothing outside of us that we can point to as the external reality of love, no electromagnetic waves passing through droplets, and no other physical phenomena. Yet love is among our most powerful experiences, and one of our strongest motivators. So are hate, fear, anger, and joy. None of our emotions exists in the external world, they're all created by us as part of our internal experience. Looking at it in the terms I've been using, Reality B is our internal response to Reality A.

Here's the problem: Our internal experience is triggered by external realities, or the perception of external realities, but we don't always perceive external realities as they actually are, but rather as our internal experience tells us they are. That's okay when we're looking at rainbows and experiencing the beauty and wonder of them. It's not okay when we make life changing decisions, manage our relationships, spend our money, start businesses, lead others into war, pass laws, make judgments in court, or try to manage our health, based on false perceptions of reality and internal experiences that are not consistent with the factuality of Reality A.

Con men, sales people, politicians, advertisers, advocates for all kinds of causes, and all manner of others depend on our human tendency to respond to our internal experiences as if they accurately reflected the external reality. They spend a lot of time, thought, and effort helping you construct a favorable experience of them (getting you to trust them) so that they can have their way with you. Often their "way" isn't what you expected or wanted, and isn't at all in your best interests. It's in cases like these that you need to be aware that your internal experience isn't necessarily reality, even if it seems to be and if you want it to be. Important decisions (decisions affecting your quality of life and well being) must be Reality A-based, or they'll be at best disappointing, and at worst life-threatening or costly in other ways.

So, it's critically important to be able to make distinctions between Reality A and our internal experiences. We don't want to eliminate our internal experiences, not even the ones that aren't fact-based; they make us human, and provide much of what's valuable and beautiful in life. But, important decisions and plans absolutely *must* be Reality A-based, even when our internal experiences are inconsistent or contradictory.

But how? When a flawed Reality B *feels* real and we unconsciously cling to the false reality of it, how can we anchor ourselves in Reality A without losing the value and wonder of our internal experience?

Well, as long as you can distinguish between Reality A and your internal experience (Reality B), then no harm no foul. For instance, can't you know that rainbows are in actuality nothing more than bent electromagnetic energy, yet still hold and enjoy the experience of their beauty? Sure you can, and you should. Can't you know that the experience of love is created within you and your loved ones, and has no external reality, yet still deeply love those near and dear to you, and be loved by them? Sure you can, and you should. But when the stakes are high, and you're making life-altering decisions, you'd better get your Reality B in tune with Reality A, or there'll be trouble.

The two-question technique gets you there.

———

So, those are the dozen distortions. I hope you've taken my advice seriously and thought through each of them and how it operates within you. Furthermore, I hope you've taken the time and effort to re-experience at least one example of each of them from your own life (or imagination), and applied the two-question technique to it to experience each one in a new, more effective, more Reality A-based way.

I want to make one more point about the two-question technique. If you consciously and diligently practice the two-question technique in real time, as the dozen distortions crop up in your life, it will first become a two-question *habit*, and sooner or later (probably sooner), the two questions will drop away, and it will become your basic nature (a habit of being) to want to know more and be open to all possibilities. At that point you'll no longer need the two questions because the attitudes of curiosity and openness will have become an innate part of who you are.

Which leads us to habits of being.

CHAPTER 4

Habits of Being

How Your Personality Can Block You

This chapter isn't "different from" the previous chapter, it's "in addition to," meaning that I'm not shifting subjects, but rather going to greater depth. I'll still be talking about habits of mind, but the deeper kind, the habits of being – think of them *as* personality habits – that are more deeply anchored in your unconscious self, more difficult to discover, more subtle in their operation, and more difficult to shift. As you'll see, the interplay of habits of thinking (which was the focus of the previous chapter) with this chapter's more deeply anchored personality habits reflects the interplay and interconnectedness of the brain itself. It all works together, seamlessly, and the distinction between "thinking" and "being" is actually artificial. They both arise from the same source, and like your arms and legs, they're different, but they're all parts of the same body, and they collectively cause you to function the way you do.

This chapter will help you answer three questions:

- What are personality habits and where do they come from?
- Which of your personality habits are blocking your entrepreneurial thinking?
- What can you do about them?

My fear for you in this chapter is that you won't like it. My fear is that you'll skim it, not like what you see, and skip to the next chapter. Or maybe you'll actually read it carefully, think, "Got it," and also go on to the next chapter without engaging in the internal discovery it asks of you. If you do that, if you're intimidated by the work it requires, impatient, or simply don't see the benefit in this particular form of self-discovery, you'll miss out on some of the most valuable insights people can learn about themselves. Your most deeply hidden blockages will remain deeply hidden, therefore unknown to you, and they'll sabotage you when you most need to succeed. And you won't have a clue why it's happening. You'll blame others, or circumstances, or even yourself, all the while being puzzled about what did or didn't happen. And your pattern will repeat, cause unknown, into the future.

So my request of you is that you take this chapter seriously. It's worth your time and effort, so commit to it. Be open to its possibilities. Dig into its practices with all the zeal you can muster, and see what comes out the other end. You'll be glad you did.

What Are Personality Habits (Habits of Being) and Where Do They Come From?

Do you know someone who is shy, intelligent, kind, and generous? Do you know someone who is aggressive, mean-spirited, and argumentative? Do you know someone who is bland, boring, and a loner? All those characteristics, and many more, are personality habits, and they make each of us a distinct and unique individual. Optimism is a personality habit, and so is pessimism. And so are procrastination, perfectionism, bullying, conflict avoidance, skepticism, compassion, competitiveness, a sense of responsibility, ambition, honesty, dishonesty, and a limitless number of others, all of them running unconsciously in our heads and making us who we are, and all of them contributing to or blocking our success.

Personality habits are important because not only do they influence your Reality B, they also influence the ways you interact with others, how you make decisions, and the manner in which you behave and take action. If you're going to be an effective business leader and entrepreneur, your habits of being need to be appropriate to the situations you encounter.

These deep-seated drivers of our thoughts and behavior seem to be in part genetic, but mostly learned. Either way, they show up in our earliest days. It happens without our knowing it, and these habits persist throughout our lives unless we become aware of them and choose to do something about them. Let me show you how habits of being typically develop using the example of a brother and sister. The brother and sister are real, but I'll respect their privacy and call them Jerry and Susan.

Jerry and Susan's father was a complex man. He was angry much of the time, but he had a soft spot for the helpless and for the underdog. When Jerry was a tiny child, probably around the time he was potty-trained, maybe earlier, and certainly earlier than he can remember, he found that he couldn't resist or rebel against his father under any circumstances. If he did, it aroused his father's instant anger, and probably earned Jerry a spanking. Jerry was afraid of his father; he loved him, but was deeply, deeply fearful of his anger, and would go to great lengths not to provoke it.

So Jerry, without thinking about it (how could he, he was under two years old?) unconsciously learned that he could prevent the threat of a spanking and reduce his fear by avoiding and withdrawing. He never opposed his father, and when dad's anger threatened, Jerry held his tongue, and withdrew. Later, he found that he didn't have to withdraw or avoid his father physically, he could avoid and withdraw internally. It became his pattern of behavior with his father. And later it became his pattern of behavior with any strong personality in his life. And even later it became his pattern of behavior in any situation where real or imagined conflict and anger might occur. And now, it's his innate habit of conflict avoidance, and it's often a counterproductive one. When the situation calls for Jerry to stand his ground and engage with other people to get something done, Jerry avoids and withdraws (internally). And he does it automatically, habitually, with no conscious awareness that he's doing it.

The early childhood pattern became the unconscious way that Jerry dealt with what he perceived as strong personalities and situations, real or imagined, that held the threat of conflict. The pattern shifted over the years, became the adult version of the little child, but remained his habitual way of dealing with things. It's more complex than that, of course, and there are many other drivers of Jerry's personality, some of which are quite effective. For instance, he's patient, understanding, readily sees other people's points of view, and has a first rate mind for strategy, among many other virtues. But he's predominantly driven, in times of stress, by avoidance and withdrawal, and he's not even aware of it. It's just the way he is.

The point is that Jerry's patterns took shape in his very early life, became unconscious behaviors of mind and action, shifted a little in response to his later experiences, but basically stayed the same and had a lot to do with shaping him as a person. The little boy who avoided and withdrew from his father's anger is still the internal little boy who "drives" Jerry's life now. Psychiatrists know all about this, and it's the basis for much of their therapy.

Jerry's sister, Susan, had the same father, but she developed differently. Dad had a soft spot for little girls, and Susan quickly (and also at an age so early that she has no memory of it) learned a successful way of coping. Instead of withdrawing, she turned on the charm, and became helpful to her father in any way she could. That completely disarmed him and turned off his anger. She derived a sense of power and control from it. She never developed a fear-based response. She learned that she could manage her circumstances by appealing to her father through charm and helpfulness.

That pattern persisted, and today's adult version of it has Susan developing cooperative relationships, networking, and helping other people succeed. It's more complex than that for Susan, too, and she has some ineffective habits of being. For instance, she's a bit narcissistic, she jumps to unwarranted assumptions quickly, and she tends to take the easy way when a more difficult path might yield better results. But the little girl who charmed and helped her way into her father's good graces is still the internal little girl who "drives" her life now.

We all – every one of us – have our own versions of Jerry's and Susan's early years and a comparable development of our own habits of being. The key points to keep in mind are these:

Much of your thinking and behavior are driven by deeply held, mostly unconscious, patterns of thought and behavior that had their origins in your earliest years. Depending on your circumstances, these patterns (your personality habits) either help or hinder you in your quest for success.

To increase your effectiveness in life and your entrepreneurial success you must identify the habits that block you, and convert them into more effective habits.

Personality Habits Are Often Obvious to Others, But Invisible to Ourselves

Personality habits are deeply ingrained and you don't pay much attention to them because they're automatic, they operate unconsciously, and they seem normal and right. They're like your bones; you can't see them, and you don't notice them, but they shape you and everything you do, and they also limit everything you do. You know about your bones, but you don't pay them much attention. You can pay attention to them any time you want, but if they're not broken or diseased, why would you? Just let them do what they do, and go on about your life.

Personality habits are a lot like that. If you habitually avoid conflict, as Jerry does, you don't pay much attention to that habit. It's just the way you are, and that's how you do things. Most likely, you're not even aware of it. If things occasionally don't work out the way you expect, you wouldn't make the connection between the event and your personality; it's *that* invisible, especially in the moment it's happening. If your conflict avoidance is brought to your attention, your unconscious mind, responding to your me-bias, will reframe it, and you'll see yourself as diplomatic and agreeable, not as a conflict avoider. For another example, if it's brought to your attention that you're aggressive and impulsive, your unconscious mind will reframe that idea and convince you that you're assertive not aggressive, and decisive not impulsive, and that's just fine; it's just the way you are.

You may see the habit as a weakness or a strength, but "it's okay," or "it's no big deal," and anyway, "it's just the way I am." And again, most likely, you're not even aware of it. When things occasionally don't work out for you, you wouldn't normally make the connection between the event and being aggressive and impulsive, or in Jerry's case, conflict avoidant.

You *need* to become aware, and you *need* to make the connections between your personality habits and the events in your life when they're not working out as you want and expect them to. If you want to be a true entrepreneur and a more successful human being, you need to be aware when your habits of being are blocking you, and you need to do something about them. So the first task is awareness; you need to identify the habits of being that are blocking your entrepreneurship.

Easier said than done, eh? If all these habits are unconscious and automatic, and therefore invisible to you as you live your life (and make your mistakes), just how do you become aware of them? You do it by looking at your own history, focusing on your unsuccessful experiences. You do it by identifying disappointing situations you have personally experienced, and drilling down to find out what it was about you that blocked you from making the most of the situation.

Remember, as I said at the outset of this book, the problem is never the business, or the conditions, or anything else. The problem is you. Most people, when confronted with their failures, come up with all kinds of "reasons" for their failure. They rationalize, and they don't even know they're doing it. Those "reasons" are nothing but excuses. They bubble up from the unconscious mind, which doesn't want you to think of yourself as anything less than great, or the negative attitude that doesn't want you to think you're great. It's a blaming mentality that wants all the problems in life to be caused by some external force, anything to avoid having to admit that "I failed" and to find a way to lay the cause of failure at some other doorstep.

So accept it. Whatever disappointment you've experienced, and whatever failure has happened on your watch, it's on you. That's the beginning of your personal discovery process – deciding to learn what it was *about you* that resulted in disappointing results and unanticipated consequences.

Why Would You Want to Change?

Converting your personality habits can feel like changing your personality, and most of us don't want to do that. To our unconscious minds, different equals bad and similar equals good. So, if I ask you to change some of your personality habits, your unconscious mind thinks I'm asking you to become, first of all, something you're not, and secondly, something bad, undesirable, or less than you are now.

If that's true, and it is, why would an aggressive person want to become weaker? Why would an optimist want to become negative? Why would a compassionate person want to become hard-hearted? Why would a considerate, peaceful person want to generate conflict and opposition? Why would a skeptic want to become gullible? Why would a competitive person want to become a loser? And on and on. For each personality habit in our personalities there is an opposite, and the opposites don't feel good to us. We don't want to be that way because our way feels better, normal, and right. But is it?

So, I'm not going to insist that you change. But, if you're willing, I am going to help you discover for yourself the personality habits that aren't working for you, give you a way to convert them into habits of your own design that *will* work for you, and leave the choice up to you. You, not I, will decide whether or not to commit to a change. And then you, not I, will make the change...or not. It's all on you. I'm just a helper.

To return to the questions above: Why would an aggressive person want to become weaker? He wouldn't. But he would want to become smarter and more creative, and channel his aggressiveness into productive actions when the situation calls for it. Why would an optimist want to become negative? She wouldn't. But she would want to understand the difference between optimism and realism when the situation calls for it. Why would a compassionate person want to become hard-hearted? He wouldn't. But he would want to apply his compassion appropriately, for instance, when making a decision that might bring harm or discomfort to a few, but which would bring greater benefit to a much larger population. Why would a competitive person want to become a loser? She wouldn't. But she would want to accept a lesser short-term result in favor of a better (and winning) long-term result. These are examples of seeing situations (and yourself) from another point of view, and also of being objective (reality over perception) about yourself.

The only one who can make valid judgments about you is you. But if you're like most of us, you'll need a little help.

And now it's time to do just that. We'll start with self-discovery.

Which of Your Personality Habits Are Blocking You? A Process for Self-Discovery

Here (below) is a process for discovering the personality habits that tend to block or diminish your success. By the way, *and this is important,* as you search for the personality habits that get in your way, you'll also notice that habits of *thinking* – the dozen distortions – will show up as well. In fact you'll probably discover the dozen distortions first, because they're less deeply anchored in your unconscious mind, less hidden from your awareness, and you've already put significant time and attention to learning about them and how they operate within you. That's as it should be because you want to fully explore *all* the habits of mind that habitually contribute to your disappointments in life. But now you're focusing on personality habits, so be sure to follow the process thoroughly, so that it will reveal to you the ones that block you. In other words, don't stop when you uncover habits of thinking (the dozen distortions), but stick with the process and "go deeper" until you've discovered any and all personality habits that were blocking you. You'll see how to do this as you read through the details of the discovery process.

First let me give you an overview so you'll know where we're headed.

Discovery Process Overview

1. Create a list of experiences from your life in which you failed, were disappointed about something significant, or experienced significant unintended consequences. This is your "bad news" list.

2. Select one of those experiences and mentally re-live it as vividly as you can.

3. List all of the reasons that explain why the experience was not as successful as you intended or expected it to be.

4. Probe those reasons to discover the habits of mind that contributed to the failure, disappointment, or inability to anticipate the consequences that happened. Probe deeply in order to go beyond the dozen distortions (habits of thinking) and discover if you have any personality habits that contributed to your disappointment.

5. Look for your patterns and priorities, and write the answer to this question: What habits got in my way, and how did they interfere with my success?

6. Select another experience from your bad news list, and do steps 2–5 again. Continue to do this until the results become repetitious and you have revealed which of the dozen distortions and which personality traits habitually block you, and under what circumstances they block you.

7. Create your prioritized "e-blockers list" containing the dozen distortions and personality habits that block your entrepreneurial thinking.

Now let's work through the process one step at a time.

Step 1: Create a "bad news list" containing the experiences in your life that were significant disappointments or outright failures.

What's the starting point for unearthing the habits of being that block you?

The starting point is you. Your life. Your experiences. The parts of your personal history when things went wrong, or when they turned out in unexpected, unwelcome ways. It's the failures, disappointments, misfortunes, wrong expectations, and big bets that didn't work out for you, that hold the secrets to what's blocking your entrepreneur's mind.

The first step is to make a list of things that went wrong or fell short of your expectations over the course of your life – call it your bad news list. By the way, forces of nature, diseases, acts of God, and other uncontrollable situations should be included in your list because, even though they were beyond your control, you still had to deal with them when they occurred. Entrepreneurial thinking, unblocked by flawed habits of mind, would have enabled you to deal with your bad news experiences more successfully than was the case when the situations actually happened. You might have minimized the damage, and sometimes even thrived in the face of the adversity.

So take a few minutes to write down a list of the times, experiences, events in your life that didn't turn out as you wanted or expected them to; all your disappointments, big and small. Include your failures, departures from what you expected, and goals that you didn't reach, or that you reached, but turned out not to have been the right goals. List all the negative experiences in your life in which you played an active role, or were the victim of circumstances beyond your control. Even major successes that fell short of your expectations, or that you felt were undeserved, and were therefore disappointments, should be included. These experiences don't have to be in the field of business. Failures and disappointments in any aspect of your life will reveal the habits that didn't work for you in those situations.

If you can't list at least a dozen or two disappointing situations from your past, you're either not trying, or your me-bias is working overtime, or you're only two years old and don't *have* much of a past.

Okay, go make your list.

Step 2: Select an experience from your bad news list and mentally re-live that experience using the "8-sense experience" technique.

The experience you select could be an outright failure, an achievement that fell short of your goals, an important prediction or expectation that didn't pan out as you thought it would, or any other situation that didn't turn out as you thought it would or wanted it to, or that you dealt with poorly. If there's an experience that you find you really don't want to deal with, or has some other strong negative energy or unpleasant emotion connected with it, that's the one you should pick first because it's sure to reveal more about your blockages than your less troubling experiences.

Re-live the experience you selected, in detail, the 8-sense way. The 8-sense experience is fully described in Attachment B at the end of this book, and you should study it. In a nutshell, it's this: Your mind takes in information by way of the five senses of sight, hearing, touch, taste, and smell. It further uses thoughts, emotions, and bodily sensations to interpret and "make sense" of the world, and to create your internal Reality B. The five senses, plus the three ways we make sense of what our senses tell us, add up to an 8-sense experience. You have an 8-sense *re-*experience by visualizing a past event as vividly and in as much detail as you can, remembering all the sights, sounds, textures, smells, and tastes, as well as the thoughts, emotions, and bodily sensations that are associated with the experience.

Take your time with this 8-sense re-experience; make it as vivid as possible in your mind.

Step 3: Create a "diagnostic ladder" showing the reasons the experience was not as successful as you intended or expected it to be.

While the re-experience is fresh and vivid in your mind, immediately complete a diagnostic ladder, which is another tool that will help you penetrate deeply into the layers of your unconscious mind, where your habits of being reside. The diagnostic ladder is an adaptation of a similar tool presented in

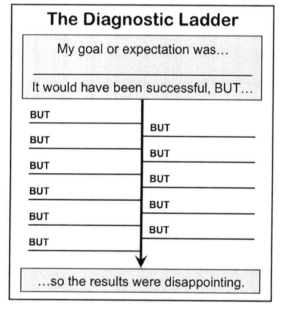

Michael Ray's insightful book, *The Highest Goal.*

The diagnostic ladder asks you to identify the goal you were trying to achieve or the expectation that fell short, and then, on the "rungs" of the "ladder" to fill in the reasons that you failed or fell short of your expectations. You'll probably find it easy to fill in three or four reasons that explain the disappointment, and you'll want to stop there, but don't stop. Push on and force yourself to fill in *all* of the blanks, even if you have to invent reasons you might not feel are quite right. The reason you have to fill in all eleven blanks, even if you have to make up some answers, and even if you are certain there were only one or two or three reasons, is that it pushes you past your conscious, top-of-mind thinking, and past your rationalizations, and more fully engages your unconscious mind.

Imagining answers, or in this case making up reasons for failure, can seem silly or misleading, but it actually helps you penetrate your unconscious mind and lead to important (and true) discoveries. So fill in all eleven blanks.

Step 4: Probe the reasons to discover the habits of mind that blocked you, using the "repeating question" technique. Probe deeply in order to go beyond the dozen distortions (habits of thinking) and reveal the personality habits that contributed to your disappointment.

This step is the heart of the practice, but it can be tricky to get right. Have a pen and paper handy to keep track of your findings.

Pick one of the "but" reasons from the diagnostic ladder and explore it thoroughly, probing for the personality habits that got in your way. You have to ignore superficial excuses and "dig deep' into your conscious and unconscious thinking and behavior to get at the real blockages. This can be difficult because your mind may want to stop at the first thing you uncover, for instance one of the dozen distortions, when in actuality, the underlying, and real, causes of the blockage may be some aspect of your personality.

Use the "repeating question technique" to probe each "but" reason. The repeating question technique is described in detail in Attachment C at the end of this book. Please study it carefully and pay close attention to the example.

In a nutshell, the repeating question technique is this: Ask yourself, "What is it about this "but" reason that blocked me?" Jot down your answer with key words or phrases that capture the essence of your answer. Then pick one of the key words or phrases (one that has some energy or importance to it, or one that you'd rather avoid), and ask the same question about this idea, "What is it about [key word or phrase] that was blocking me? Again, jot down the key words or phrases that come to you. Continue "drilling down" with the repeating question until you sense that you have reached the heart of the matter. You'll feel it as some kind of "aha" or feeling of relief, a satisfaction, rather than a sense of wanting to move on to the next thing.

If you feel stumped or blocked at any level of repeating questions, it's a sign that you're unconsciously avoiding something. You'll need to break through that unconscious resistance. Push through it by re-asking the repeating question, and if necessary, speculating about answers that might be true of others, even if you don't think they're true for you. Again, jot down the key words/phrases. At some point, you'll have that "aha" and you'll intuitively know that you've discovered what you were looking for.

Occasionally, you may still find yourself blocked and unable to break through. That's okay because you're going to be probing other "but" reasons from the diagnostic ladder, and, even though you didn't get all the way to the bottom of this one, it's good preparation (especially for your unconscious mind) for the next ones you probe. Be patient with yourself.

Sometimes, you'll have a sense of completion without having discovered a personality trait responsible for the disappointment. That's because, in that instance, personality may not have been the problem. It may have been one or more of the dozen distortions that blocked your success. "Sense of completion" is the key here. Sense of completion means an "aha" feeling, a sense of satisfaction, or some other positive response. If you feel blocked, resistant, are anxious about going further and are experiencing negative thoughts, intuitions, emotions, or bodily sensations that make you want to avoid further probing, it's a sign that you haven't gotten to the bottom of your probing, and you need to persist with the repeating questions. The signs can be subtle, so pay attention to your state of mind as you do this probing, and stick with it when your mind wants to resist going further.

I realize that this is all vague and touchy-feely. It has to be because this practice works differently in different people, and it relies on intuition and the unique associations that live in your mind, and your mind only. You have to get in touch with your own inner workings, and tune yourself in to the subtle ones, the ones you usually don't notice, or which you ignore. The unconscious mind wants to stay unconscious, so you have to pay close attention to yourself and learn the ways that yours communicates with you. The language of the unconscious mind consists of emotions, bodily sensations, impressions, and intuitions. You'll have your own patterns to pay attention to. I can give you some hints, but because I don't know you, I can't tell you what your patterns might be. Fortunately, the more you engage in this practice, the better you'll become at doing it, and no small thing, the better you'll understand yourself.

When you've probed each "but" reason and have a solid sense of completion about it, go on to the next one that draws your attention, or that you want to avoid.

Although you had to list at least eleven "but" reasons, you probably don't have to probe all of them. When do you know you're done? When the results of your probing become repetitious. You'll need to probe at least five "but" reasons to be sure you're not missing any important habits of mind, so five is the minimum. When you've probed five or more "but" reasons, and the same habits of mind crop up again and again, you'll know you've mined this bad news experience for all of its secrets. So keep at it until either repetition sets in, or you've probed all eleven reasons, but don't let yourself probe less than five.

At the end of this step, you should have five or more sheets of paper with key words and phrases scribbled on them, one sheet for each "but" reason you probed.

Step 5: Look for your patterns and priorities, and write the answer to this question: "What habits got in my way, and how did they interfere with my success?"

Review each of your key words and phrases sheets, looking for personality habits and dozen distortions that show up frequently, or if they only show up rarely, have major negative effects. Sorry, I wish I had a formula for this process, but the only thing that seems to work is your own powers of observation and your intuition. [Interesting, isn't it, that even here, when you're exploring your unconscious mind, the unconscious mind itself turns out to be your best tool?]

One warning: When you're looking for your patterns, don't merely count words. Yes, pay attention to the numbers; if a key word or phrase crops up many times, that means something, but so does your internal sense of importance, your intuition about yourself.

Take another blank sheet of paper and write a quick note about what you've discovered about yourself and the habits of mind that blocked you when you had this bad news experience. Be specific, and be especially sure to write down the ones that seemed to have created the strongest distortions of reality and contributed most strongly to the disappointing results of this experience. Attach this sheet to the front of your key words and phrases sheets.

Step 6: Go on to another experience on your bad news list, and do steps 2–5 again. Continue to do this until the results become repetitious and you have revealed all the personality habits that habitually block you.

At this point you've thoroughly explored one experience from your life that didn't work out the way you wanted it to, and you've gotten a lot of valuable insights about the way your mind works and how your personality can get in your way. But you can't rely on one experience, or even several experiences out of a lifetime of experiences, to reveal the patterns – the habits of mind – that block your entrepreneur's mind. You have to explore many experiences. How many? I don't know, but you will. When the exploration of your bad news experiences gets repetitious, when you see the same habits of mind repeatedly, across many experiences, getting in the way of success, then you'll know how you block yourself.

In general, for most people, exploring five or ten experiences from relatively recent years will reveal their consistent patterns, and allow them to identify the main ways they're blocking themselves. So, think in terms of reviewing a half-dozen to a dozen bad news experiences.

The last discovery step is to put it all together and begin a plan for unblocking yourself.

Step 7: Create your prioritized "e-blockers list" containing the personality habits that block your entrepreneurial thinking.

When you've completed exploring the necessary number of bad news experiences, you'll have many sheets of paper for each experience. That's your raw material. Let it sit for a day or so (to allow your unconscious mind to integrate it all) and then go back to your note sheets and put it all together in the form of a prioritized list of habits of mind, each of which has played a role in blocking your entrepreneur's mind; we'll call it your "e-blockers List."

What do I mean by prioritized? The first item on your list should be the habit that had the greatest negative impact on your thoughts and actions across the greatest number of bad news life experiences. What's "negative impact"? Distorted perceptions of reality. Beliefs that were wrong, or at least uncertain. Emotional reactions that clouded your perceptions and shaped ineffective or erroneous thoughts and actions from you. Personality characteristics that weren't appropriate, meaning that they clouded your perceptions, limited your willingness to take the appropriate actions, or motivated you to take inappropriate actions. All the stuff we talked about in the previous chapters.

Your e-blockers list, if you're like most of us, will be a mix of habits of thinking and habits of being. They might even be habits that are normally useful, but which, in your bad news experiences, blocked you and produced disappointing results. The top item on the list will be the habit of thinking or personality trait, that, across many bad news experiences, was the most significant contributor to the disappointing results, or said another way, blocked you more than any other habit on the list. Again, I can't give you objective criteria for choosing your most significant blockers because everyone's mind works in its own patterns; no formula works for everyone. I can assure you, however, that'll you know them when you see them.

Last, but not least, go back over your e-blockers list and identify each habit on the list as either a habit of thinking or personality habit. That's important because the process for converting habits of thinking into supporting habits is the two-question habit, which I covered in the previous chapter. It differs from and is simpler than the process for shifting your more deeply anchored personality habits, which I'll tell you about next.

Your e-blockers list is the end of your discovery process, and the beginning of the what-are-you-going-to-do-about-it part of this book. The great thing about this discovery practice is that, merely by getting deeply engaged in it (not simply going through the motions, but really "getting into it") the practice will change you for the better. Your unconscious mind pays attention to what you're doing even when what you're doing focuses on the unconscious mind itself, and it'll begin to think differently, and better, simply as a result of doing all this work. So you're already taking big steps along the path toward true entrepreneurial thinking.

What Can You Do About the Personality Habits that Block You?

Fortunately, it's possible to change personality habits, even the deep seated ones that seem inborn, the ones that seem so, you. Obstructive personality habits can be converted into productive ones, and the new habits that you need for success can be learned.

But you can't simply "act" differently. You have to change at the deep, unconscious, *real you* level. Some say "fake until you make it," but that simply disguises your underlying habits with artificial behavior in the hope that the artificiality will wear off and the behavior will eventually become genuine. It doesn't work. All you're doing is adding a new habit, the habit of acting. The underlying habits that the acting is attempting to camouflage still remain in place, and they'll reassert themselves, often at the worst possible time, when the stakes are important and stress is high.

For instance, don't you know people who are amazingly positive, whatever the situation? And can't you immediately see which of them are genuinely positive, and which have learned positivity techniques, and think that makes them positive? The genuinely positive ones take on the world with an innate zest and genuine confidence, while the others seem strained, unreal, and stressed, all the while smiling a dazzling smile and congratulating themselves on how very positive they are. You don't really trust them, do you? And unconsciously, they don't trust themselves. Their unconscious minds know the truth, and it shows; they can't hide it.

So, instead of *acting* positive, confident, assertive, innovative, or any other desirable habit of mind, you need to learn how to build a foundation of supportive unconscious habits so that a productive attitude naturally emerges. This way you don't have to *act* positive, confident, assertive, or innovative, etc.) because you *become truly* positive, and never have to act again. And that's where you're headed in this chapter, but before you get into the process by which you convert your blocking habits into supportive habits, let me say a few more words about those habits.

Firstly, while you have scores, maybe hundreds, of personality habits that collectively form your personality and shape your character, most people find that only a very few of them are important barriers to their success, and only in certain situations. Two, three, or four (rarely more) of your personality habits will be the ones that are getting in your way. The point here is that even though you have hundreds of personality habits, you'll only have to work on a small number of them. So, it's not an insurmountable task.

The second point is that this whole process is you-focused. If everyone were the same, I'd have offered a simple formula, and advised you to follow that formula. But you are you, and you're not like anyone else. So your solutions have to be you-focused because anything else won't work. That means you'll have to explore your own inner landscape, and if you've ever done anything like this before, or been close to others who have, you know it can be tricky and sometimes challenging. Furthermore, our minds are structured so that we see ourselves in an artificially favorable light. I call it the "me-bias" because it creates a lot of unconscious self-deception, in the form of beliefs about yourself, such as: "I know what's real, and I see it more clearly than you," and personal blind spots such as: "I'm a great salesman," or "I'm really good with people," when in fact you might not be any of those things, all the while fervently believing you are. So, you not only have to discover what's true for you, you have to be open to a lot of surprising news about yourself, and it's sometimes stuff you don't want to know. The me-bias works the other way, too. Some of you will have some falsely negative views of yourselves, such as: "I'm not very creative," or "I'm a lousy salesman," or "I'm not a 'detail' person." Positive or negative, false beliefs about ourselves and the habits of being they support, can be barriers against a lot of life's good stuff, not the least of which is entrepreneurial talent.

The third point I want to make before you embark on this journey is this: Don't expect it to be difficult. But don't expect it not to be. It will be what it is for you. Some people breeze through the process easily and quickly. Some work through it laboriously, stressed out and frustrated every step of the way. And some just don't get it, and give up. The vast majority of normal, healthy people get a lot of "aha" moments about themselves, find some parts of the process difficult, and some parts easy, and look back on the journey as worthwhile and successful.

The fourth point is you're in control. You don't have to do any of this if you don't want to. And you can shift it around to work better if some part of the process isn't working for you. This whole book is simply a guideline built on mind/brain science and practices that have worked for others. But you're not others, and some parts of it may not work exactly right for you. So change it. Isn't that what entrepreneurs do? When something doesn't work, they do something else; they create a different way to get the job done. In fact, that's an important lesson in entrepreneurial thinking. So be open to other possibilities as you work through the process. As long as you follow the basic principles we've discovered and described in this book, you'll be okay.

And finally, don't expect a transformation. I don't believe in transformations. Transformation works for caterpillars and tadpoles, but not for people. Because the process is you-focused, and because *you* are driving it, the results will be consistent with who you are, and will reflect your own kind of person. I find that people who are successful come out the other side of the process, not saying "I'm a whole new person," but rather saying something like, "I'm the same person I've always been, but things (my life, my relationships, my business) are working better for me."

The Habit Conversion Process

The essence of habit conversion is to take advantage of the mind's natural habit formation process, but to do it consciously, with the intention of replacing habits that aren't working for you. The essential elements of consciously forming a new habit are attention and repetition. You put your attention on the new habit you want to develop, and you practice it diligently until it becomes part of you. You saw a simple version of it with the two-question habit introduced in the previous chapter to deal with the dozen distortions, but it's a bit more challenging for personality habits.

You can't simply identify a bad personality habit and decide not to do it any more. You have to replace it with a new habit, one that's compatible with the rest of your habits of mind. There's a saying, "What you resist persists." It's true. Resisting a bad habit keeps that habit in your conscious and unconscious mind. It actually reinforces the undesirable habit. For example, if I tell you, "Don't think of a pink elephant," what happens? You think of a pink elephant; you can't help it. The harder you try not to think of a pink elephant, the longer the pink elephant stays in your mind. If you want to eliminate the image of the pink elephant, you have to consciously direct yourself to think of something else. Instead of resisting the pink elephant, you replace it with, say, the image of a unicorn. Look at what just this moment happened in your own mind. Didn't the image of a unicorn flash into your mind, and for that moment, didn't the pink elephant disappear? So, the basic principle of habit conversion is this: don't try to resist or eliminate the old habit; *replace* it with something better.

Part of the problem of persistent bad habits is that they're always stimulated (triggered) by something, and that something is almost always unconscious. The way to convert a blocking habit into an effective habit is to identify the trigger and make yourself conscious of it so you can use it as an alert to tell you when to engage in new behavior to replace the old habit. After you do it enough times, the trigger will automatically and unconsciously stimulate the new habit instead of the old, and you'll have successfully converted the old habit, not by rejecting it, but by replacing it.

Let me illustrate by continuing the example of Jerry, whom you met in an earlier chapter. Recall that Jerry had developed the lifelong personality habit of conflict avoidance, based on the way he learned as a child to cope with his father's anger. As you may remember, over time as Jerry grew into manhood, his avoidance of his father's anger became the unconscious pattern – a personality habit – for the way he dealt with all real and imagined conflicts in his life.

Every time Jerry got into a confrontation with someone, or imagined that a confrontation might develop, he became tense and got a tight feeling in his gut.

Whenever the tight feeling happened, Jerry would relieve the tension by moving away from the situation, or if he couldn't physically move away, he would withdraw mentally by numbing out, becoming confused, or simply going blank. Others saw it as changing the subject, going along to get along, or disengaging from the discussion by going silent, none of which helped move the situation forward to a useful solution or decision. His behavior was so habitual that he no longer paid attention to the tightness in his gut, and didn't even realize that he was avoiding real or imagined conflict in an unconsciously habitual way. If you pointed it out to him, he simply rationalized his behavior by saying, "Well, I just didn't have anything to contribute to the discussion so I moved away," or "I was very interested in the discussion, and I could see merit in both sides of the argument, but I had no position on it, so I just listened."

When Jerry used the discovery process and found that conflict avoidance was at the top of his e-blocker list, his first reaction was shock and embarrassment. His second reaction was, "I've got to do something about that." When I helped him mentally recall and re-live several situations in which his conflict avoidance was an important contributor to his failure or disappointment, he became aware that, in every instance, he always felt a tension in his gut just before his conflict avoidance habit took charge of him. That gave us a way to change this long-standing and unproductive habit of mind. He devised a way to "avoid his avoidance". Rather than disengaging and withdrawing, he would simply ask questions. He'd use curiosity and questioning to stay engaged and contribute to a positive result rather than merely escaping from the situation. He had a natural curiosity, so asking questions gave him a non-conflictual way to interrupt the old habit and stay engaged. And in those few instances when conflict actually did result, his conscious awareness and intention to stay engaged, combined with the questioning approach, gave him a useful and productive way to work his way through the conflict.

In short, he primed himself to notice his gut tension so he could use it as an alert to short-circuit his disengagement and to trigger a better way of behaving in a potentially conflictual situation. When real-time situations happened, he was able to notice the gut alert, and consciously shift his old habit into the new, questioning, behavior. Eventually, with both real-life and mental practice, the gut tension became an unconscious trigger to the questioning habit instead of the withdrawing one. In the long run (a few weeks) the old habit disappeared because his new habit eliminated the sense of threat in these situations, which eliminated the tension. It became natural for him to become productively involved in finding solutions and helping to eliminate the potential for conflict. His withdrawal and avoidance shifted into engagement and problem solving. Is it any wonder that his life improved from that point onward?

I hope you find it reassuring that this whole process depends on the natural ways your mind functions. You don't have to learn anything new, you just have to take advantage of what your mind already does by nature, and do it consciously rather than unconsciously. All you do is consciously notice your triggers and intentionally move into a new behavior of your own creation, one that's in tune with who you are, and that will be more productive than the old habit. Your mind is already equipped to form and re-form habits. All I'm doing is helping you learn how to do it consciously, deliberately, and in service of your own success, rather than as an unconscious response to your lifelong conditioning.

For many people, the habit conversion process can be a bit tricky, so I'm going to ask you to ease into it. The first thing I'd like you to do is look at the overview below, which summarizes the process. It'll give you the lay of the land for what we'll be doing next. After that I'll walk you through each step of the process, and after that you'll begin, if you're willing, to reconstruct your own e-blocker habits so they'll serve you better.

Habit Conversion Overview

Converting your e-blocker habits

1. Select a blocker habit from your e-blocker list.
2. Select a bad news experience in which that e-blocker habit was active. Mentally re-live it the 8-sense re-experience way.

3. Identify the trigger point and establish your alert.
4. Choose a new, supportive habit.
   a. For habits of thinking (the dozen distortions) use the two-question technique.
   b. For personality habits, create a new, supportive way of being.
5. Mentally practice the new, improved habit the 8-sense pre-experience way, and engage the new habit in real-time situations whenever they occur in the ordinary course of your life.
6. Practice to completion.

You'll find that habits of thinking – the dozen distortion habits – are relatively easy to change, but that personality habits tend to be more stubborn, and require more attention and persistence to convert permanently.

That's the overview. Now let's get you engaged with the real thing. Remember, as I've said before, that you'll be clumsy with the process at first. It will feel weird and unnatural, but with practice, it'll all become comfortable and you'll get good at it. Here's the detailed process.

Step 1: Select a blocker habit from your e-blocker list

The first time you use this conversion process, select "secondary" e-blocker habits to work on. By secondary, I meant habits that contributed to your disappointments and failures, but weren't the most important habits, or the ones that "drove" the experience. These would be habits that you didn't prioritize as first, second, or third on your e-blocker list. The reason should be obvious; you'll get the best results from the conversion process after you've had some practice with it. The highest priority e-blockers are the ones that will be most important to convert, so practice on a secondary habit before taking on the ones that drive your unsuccessful experiences.

Step 2: Select a bad news experience in which that e-blocker habit was active. Mentally re-live it the 8-sense re-experience way

When you did your discovery work you explored a number of bad news experiences from your life, experiences in which things didn't turn out as you wanted or expected. Go back to your bad news experiences and pick one in which the e-blocker you selected played a role in blocking your success.

You'll need to re-live that experience as vividly as you can. As you learned in the discovery process, the 8-sense experience, or in this case, 8-sense *re*-experience, is the best way to do that. As you did before, close your eyes, relax, and mentally re-live the experience, regenerating as much as you can, in your mind, of the sights, sounds, smells, tastes, textures, thoughts, emotions, and bodily sensations that you experienced at the time of the actual experience.

Step 3: Identify the trigger point and establish your alert

While your re-experience is still vivid in your mind, look for the point at which your e-blocker habit was triggered. It'll be the point in time just before the habit took hold and locked you into your automatic way of thinking or being. This can be tricky because these triggers usually go unnoticed in real time, and they're often subtle. Also, you never know if it's a thought, emotion, or bodily sensation that's associated with the point at which the habit takes hold, so, as you're reliving the experience, you have to pay close attention to what was going on within you and around you during the moment the habit was triggered. It could be a momentary hesitancy, an instant of anxiety that you normally wouldn't notice, a spark of annoyance or irritation, a little tingle of apprehension, a flash of impatience, a hint of fear, or a thought such as "Oh, no, not again"; anything you notice about yourself, your thoughts and emotions, or even the situation around you, that occurs just before you go into the habitual behavior.

This is another of those things that's unique to you. Again, I can't give you a formula, just some hints about what to look for. The rule is that it must be something that you can prime yourself to notice so that it will alert you to stay conscious and aware and to intentionally interrupt the e-blocker habit and divert yourself into a different thinking pattern or a better way of being. In the earlier example of Jerry dealing with his conflict aversion, he always either had a strong desire to withdraw or go silent, or a "need" to be elsewhere, in either case, accompanied by tension in his gut. That tension was his signal (his alert) to stay engaged and attempt to improve the situation, rather than merely avoid it. Once he realized what his alert was, he could prime himself to notice it, and respond to it with intentional new behavior.

Having identified your alert, what do you do about it? How do you devise an improved habit of mind to take the place of the ineffective one?

Step 4: Choose a new, supportive habit

Recall that on your e-blocker list, you identified each blocker habit as either a dozen distortions habit (habit of thinking) or a personality habit (habit of being). I asked you to do that because the two kinds of habits require different conversions. As you saw in the previous chapter, the dozen distortion habits are all "fixed" by the two-question habit, which I've repeated for you below. You have to be more clever about replacing habits of being.

For dozen distortions habits, use the two-question technique

To remind you of the two-question technique, whenever you're triggered into a habit of thinking that you've decided you need to change, consciously and deliberately ask and answer the following two questions, in the order shown:

What's Reality A?
What are the facts? What do you *know* is the actual reality outside of your mind (Reality A) and, separately, what is the product of your opinion or interpretation; (your Reality B)? What do you believe that could be questioned? If necessary, quickly refer to the dozen distortions list to remind yourself about the most common ways you might be distorting your thinking.

What are the possibilities?
What else do I need to know about the situation? What are the other possibilities, even if they're highly unlikely? How would someone else see the situation?

For personality habits, create a new, supportive way of being

There's a secret to successfully converting personality habits, and it's this: The new habit must be compatible with the way your mind works, not simply some artificial and uncomfortable way of thinking or being that you have to force upon yourself. For instance, if you were to think, "I'll be just like the Dalai Lama, peaceful and positive" but your normal of habits of mind are at odds with the Dalai Lama's way, then the replacement habit won't take hold, and won't replace the old habit. It'll be like "acting" positive, when you aren't truly positive.

Think again about Jerry and his conflict aversion. The new habit for him was based on the fact that he was a genuinely curious person, with a sincere desire to help make a situation better, and his constellation of normal habits tended to support that state of mind. Real or imagined conflict threw him into withdrawal/avoidance, and because that was not his usual state of mind, made his discomfort with conflict even greater. When he primed himself to notice his gut tension alert, he used that awareness to trigger the conscious intention to "hang in there" and to do so by asking questions and working toward solutions. In other words, he took advantage of his normal, productive state of mind, curiosity and helpfulness, and used that as the foundation of his new, effective habit.

Here's a thought experiment for you that might help you understand how you might go about creating a new, more effective habit of being for yourself. Imagine that the habit of being you need to change is that you're overly impulsive. Most of your bad news experiences were driven by your impulsiveness, which causes you to jump to conclusions and act on your first thoughts rather than being more thoughtful and seeking the best course of action. Like most impulsive people, you probably trust your intuition more than your analytical thinking. You're probably not aware (if asked you might not even believe) that the best decisions are the result of a combination of intuitive and analytical thinking working in tandem. Imagine also that you've discovered that the trigger for your impulsivity is the urge to get results quickly, and the urge has a physical component, which is a bodily sensation of a pleasant sort of tingling in your solar plexus, which you've noticed takes place immediately before you make significant decisions and take action on them.

You're a naturally action-oriented person, and that's a good thing that you wouldn't want to suppress. So you use your natural bias for action as the foundation for a new, more effective habit of being than your impulsiveness. You might do that by redirecting your action bias toward finding the best possible alternative, rather than acting on the first thing that occurs to you. In other words, you redefine "action" to mean the search for the best solution, and you redefine impulsivity as the intuitive need to get the best result, rather than the need to swing into action as quickly as possible. If you try to establish the habit of "slow down and think" that'll run counter to the constellation of habits that you've built over your lifetime that compels you into (usually premature) action. You won't be able to do it. It'll feel awful to "slow down" and you'll feel like you're wasting precious time dithering about the situation; it'll feel like paralysis by analysis. But if you redirect your energy and action bias into finding the *right* solution rather than the *immediate* solution, and if you trust your whole mind – both your intuition and your analytical thinking – you'll be able to create a whole new way of making decisions, and it'll be strengthened by your action bias and your trust in your intuition (your gut).

Your thought process might go something like this:

I learned in my discovery process that most of the poor decisions I've made in my life happened when I was too impulsive, too action biased. I used to think that my intuition was reliable, and that I was a quick decision maker for that reason. But when I reviewed the poor decisions I've made in my life, it became clear that I was merely jumping to conclusions, believing them to be right. And at the time they felt right, although in most cases they later proved to have been wrong, and led, ultimately, to disappointments.

But I can't simply become a deliberate, slow, overly cautious decision maker. That would drive me crazy, and I'm not sure I could even do it. However, I *can see the possibility of redirecting my action bias into an aggressive search for the best course of action, and verify my intuition with some analytical thinking. I could look at it like this: My first and immediate decision would be to search for the best course of action, and my **second** decision would be to aggressively put that course of action into effect.*

As I think about it, I can see that I'd be converting impulsiveness into assertiveness or even aggressiveness, but thoughtful rather than careless aggressiveness. Instead of wasting time, I'd be making the best possible use of my time, and emotionally it would still feel action-based, not inert or lazy. The best part of this approach is that it feels like "me" and it takes advantage of what has always felt like one of my greatest strengths.

It's all simply a shift of perspective, isn't it? But it's a genuine shift, not an "act," and emotionally it feels right because it's true to what feels like my basic nature. That's because it meshes, rather than conflicts, with some of my other important habits of mind. It's not "transformation." It's realignment of an ineffective habit of mind so that it meshes with the effective parts of my personality and my effective habits of thinking.

Designing the best replacement habit requires a lot of willingness to be honest, open, and objective about yourself, and to allow for a lot of new possibilities that you may not have ever considered. It's all part of becoming more conscious, more aware, and more intentional about your life. It's ultimately about overcoming the normal supremacy of unconscious thinking and being.

To summarize, you'll need to devise a replacement habit that taps into your authentic personality and takes advantage of other existing, but productive habits, and you'll need to prime yourself so that when you experience the trigger, it'll alert you to consciously initiate the new, more effective way of being.

Step 5: Pre-experience (the 8-sense way) the new, improved habit

If you're like me, you're probably thinking, "How the heck can I do that? How can I create a replacement habit that meshes with my authentic personality?"

Once again, you'll need to use the 8-sense experience, in fact two of them; an 8-sense _re_-experience, followed by an 8-sense _pre_-experience. It works like this: First, you have an 8-sense re-experience of a time when your existing habit didn't work well for you. You should pick one of the same past experiences you used when you were discovering your e-blockers list because it'll be familiar to you, fresh in your mind, and you'll know what the trigger/alert was. As you're re-experiencing the event, you'll come to the point at which it was triggered. That's where the re-experience stops and the pre-experience begins. This is the point at which you switch from memory to imagination. Visualize a way you could have and should have handled the event that would have had a better result, and visualize yourself as if you had behaved this new way instead of what you actually did. In other words, visualize success instead of disappointment, and try to live it in your imagination as if you had done it in real-time, when it actually occurred in your past. You may have to try out a few different scenarios in your mind to find one that your intuition and logic tell you will work, and will also feel like "you." Remember, you need to find a new habit that will mesh with your personality, one that you believe will work, but also one that is compatible with who you are. It might take a few different pre-experiences to find one that will be authentic, and I can't tell you what that authentic one might be. I can tell you that it'll be the one that feels less awkward than the others. Anything you imagine yourself doing that's different from your old habit (the one you need to replace) will feel different and maybe somewhat strange, but the one that resonates with the authentic you will give you a sense of rightness, a sense of "this is it." Go with that. If it turns out not to be right, or if you later discover a better way of being, you can always shift to the better way as soon as you discover it. In fact, as you mentally practice the new habit, you should continually be alert for better possibilities, and adopt them as they occur to you. As you practice (see next step) you'll settle in to the way that works best for you.

Let me say a bit more about visualization and mental rehearsal to reassure you that this technique of pre-experiencing is much more than wishful thinking and "let's pretend." A pre-experience or visualization is trying something new on for size without actually risking failure or embarrassment. You'll never create a mental experience that's as intense as one you actually live, of course, but visualization using the 8-sense re-experience or pre-experience is the next best thing. The reason for using visualization at all is that you can make great progress, yet do it all in your mind where it's safe, where you can't make mistakes, and where there are no risks, no embarrassment, and no failures or negative consequences.

Let me give you an example from sports. In college, I was a diver on the varsity swimming team. The first thing my coach taught me was visualization. For every dive, without exception, I was to imagine myself performing the dive perfectly. Only after that mental rehearsal was I allowed to mount the diving board and do the dive. When learning a new dive, I practiced mentally dozens if not hundreds of times in my mind before attempting the dive for the first time. The scarier and more difficult the dive, the more I practiced it mentally before diving.

Diving is a physical habit, but any habit, physical or mental, can be imagined and practiced by visualization with no risk of failure, no embarrassment, and the more you visualize it, the more you become accustomed to it. When you finally do it for real, it feels familiar, and flows much more easily than if you tried it without mental rehearsal.

What my diving coach didn't know, and what I've learned over the years is that the 8-Sense approach works best because it engages all the senses, and all of the conscious and unconscious mental associations (head, heart, and gut) that make the internal experience, if not a real experience, at least a near-real one. Nothing is happening in the real, external world, yet, in your mind, you're establishing new neural pathways that will have real world consequences. Just as I once did when learning a new dive, you're mentally rehearsing something you've never done, so that when you actually do it, it will work for you.

Step 6: Practice to completion

When you've identified your new, replacement habit of being, then, several times daily, visualize (pre-experience) the new behavior; rehearse it in your mind. Adjust and revise it mentally whenever you feel that you need to in order to get it right. And be on the alert for real world situations to put the new habit into actual practice.

Mental practice is all well and good (necessary actually) but what you're after is results in the real world, when real-life situations occur. And that's what you'll do. Rehearse the new behavior mentally several times daily, in the safety of your mind, so that when situations occur in real life, you'll do what you've mentally rehearsed.

Real life is the acid test. If in real life the new habit needs adjusting, then adjust it. Find the behavior that works best for you, and then diligently and consciously do it at all opportunities. And continue your visualization.

How long do you do this? Do it until you do it automatically, without consciously thinking about it. At that point in time, and no sooner, it'll have become a new habit of mind, and will need no further rehearsal because it'll have become part of who you are.

If you find yourself thinking, "Now I've got it. I don't have to consciously trigger the new habit any more," it's proof that you haven't yet fully broken the old habit, just superseded it from time to time with conscious intention. The very fact that you've consciously thought about the old habit, means that it's still alive in you, and not fully replaced by the new habit. What needs to happen is that you *consciously* engage the new habit every time you're triggered, and be diligent about doing it every time. Eventually, you'll forget to put your conscious intention on it, and the new habit, with no further conscious intention, asserts itself whenever the trigger occurs. It won't occur to you to think about it, you'll automatically do it.

I can't tell you how many times people have told me, "I get it," believing that they need only decide on a new habit and be aware of the trigger, and that's all that's necessary. Just because you know the trigger and the new habit in your conscious mind, doesn't mean that it's anchored in your unconscious mind. In fact, it's not. Not until the new habit itself becomes unconscious, and your conscious mind is no longer even aware that that trigger is sliding you into the new habit, not until then is the new habit established beyond the point at which it can still snap back into your old habit. I guarantee that you'll be tempted, at the point when the new habit is familiar and easy to engage, to let it go at that, and stop practicing. Don't stop. Continue practicing until you forget about it and it becomes automatic. It's the way you were conditioned into your existing habits of mind, and it's the *only* way you'll successfully convert flawed habits into new ones that work better for you.

I have to repeat something one more time: Initially, you can expect discomfort, forgetfulness, and in some cases fear of failure or embarrassment. That's why mental practice – visualization through the 8-sense pre-experience – is so important. You get to practice in the privacy of your own mind, where there are no witnesses, no risks, and where you can experiment with no consequences, while still getting the benefits of practice and self-conditioning.

Do not shortcut this process.

One Last Thought About Habit Conversion

So far in this book, all we've been doing is to clear away the barriers to successful entrepreneurship by helping you to identify some of your most important beliefs and blocker habits so that you could learn how to think and act more realistically, more consciously, and more intentionally.

Your thinking should improve dramatically and quickly as you discover your blocking habits of mind and convert them to more productive ways of thinking and being. As you already know, it's an awkward process in the beginning but you get better at it over time. As you use the discovery and conversion processes, they, too, will become automatic and unconscious habits of mind. Stick with it, and you'll become a clear thinker with a productive personality, and it'll become your innate, basic nature, not some skill that you've adopted. It'll be a permanent upgrade of who you are; not a transformation, but a better you.

I realize that this is a lot of work. And it's challenging because you're re-engaging some of the more painful (or at least sensitive) experiences in your life, digging into some deeply buried parts of your mind, and confronting a lot of things about yourself that you'd rather not. The problem is that this is one of those things that's inherently not simple, easy, quick, and cheap. Your mind is enormously complex, and it's taken you all of your lifetime (so far) to build the habits of mind that inhabit your head, including the ones that are blocking you. It won't take you a lifetime to release your blockages and establish your entrepreneur's mind, but it will take weeks, maybe even months for some of you, and you have to *engage* in the process or it won't work. It's not positive thinking, it's not "fake it until you make it, it's not slogans or formulas, and it's not opening yourself up to the universe to make things right. It's you reshaping your mind.

If "be all you can be" has any meaning for you (as it does for me) that's what it is.

———

That's the how; how to think better as an entrepreneur, or for that matter as a better human being. Next comes the "what." As an entrepreneur, what are the contents of your mind? What, specifically, do you think about?

Read on.

Part Two: The Entrepreneur's Mind: What Goes Right?

CHAPTER 5

Entrepreneur, Know Thyself

Core Purpose, the Source of Deep Motivation

Purpose and Motivation

All the gurus of leadership and personal development recognize that every person has a powerful inner drive, usually unnoticed and unconscious, yet still influencing everything we do in life. Renowned author and lecturer Tony Robbins calls it one's sense of "ultimate destiny." Michael Gerber, pioneering business coach and author of the best-selling E-Myth books, calls it "Primary Aim." Steven Covey, best selling author of *The 7 Habits of Highly Effective People,* identifies it as a spiritual drive for meaning and contribution. Michael Ray, author of *Creativity in Business,* and creator of the Stanford University course in business creativity, calls it the "Greatest Goal." Others have different names for it, but they all recognize that it exists, and that it's an important source of motivation and power. I call it "Core Purpose."

We all have a lot of things in life that motivate us, but Core Purpose is the deepest and most meaningful. It's the source of our most enduring motivation. If you can see how your entrepreneurship contributes to accomplishing your Core Purpose, then you've made a connection that will sustain you when the going gets tough and you're tempted to quit or take the easy way out.

Everyone has a Core Purpose, and it's different for everyone. Yet most people aren't aware (a) that they even have a Core Purpose, much less what their own Core Purpose is, and (b) how important it is to live their lives in ways that are in harmony with their Core Purposes.

A deep sense of purpose, not a reaction to needs

I'm going to show you a process for discovering your Core Purpose in a moment, but first you need to know a bit about human motivation, and why Core Purpose stands apart from other kinds of motivation. Bear with me while I get a bit pedantic; it'll just take a moment.

In 1943 Abraham Maslow published a paper entitled "A Theory of Human Motivation" in which he observed that people are motivated to fulfill their needs, and those needs exist in a hierarchy in which the more basic needs must be satisfied before the higher needs can become motivators. In other words, if you're starving, you probably aren't motivated to join the country club, but if you're healthy and well-fed, and you feel safe and secure, then the need to be accepted and belong to a desirable group will emerge as strong motivators for you. The needs Maslow identified (from the most basic to the more elevated) were physiological, safety/security, love/belonging, esteem/accomplishment, self-actualization, and (added by Maslow in later years) self-transcendence. The need for self-transcendence is the domain of Core Purpose, and you'll see in a moment how it differs from the other needs and why that's important to you. Here's a summary of Maslow's hierarchy, with needs listed from the most basic at the bottom of the list, to the highest at the top:

Maslow's Hierarchy of Needs	
SELF-TRANSCENDENCE	Higher goals, outside of the self. Service to the "greater self" or humanity. Not a need but a sense of purpose. (Outer-directed)
SELF-ACTUALIZATION	The urge to "be all you can be." (Self-referenced)
ESTEEM/ACHIEVEMENT	The need for status, recognition, accomplishment. (Self-referenced)
LOVE/BELONGING	The need for affiliation with others and groups; relationships. (Self-referenced)
SAFETY/SECURITY	The need to be safe and secure. (Self-referenced)
PHYSIOLOGICAL	The need for sustenance and comfort; physical needs, such as food, shelter, etc. The so-called "survival" needs. (Self-referenced)

Maslow identified self-transcendence as the highest need, but this is where I depart from Maslow's theory. My experience in business, in the military, and in family matters, has shown me that self-transcendence is a motivator whether or not lower level needs have been satisfied. In other words, when the stakes are important, we humans will put others ahead of ourselves and make sacrifices for a greater purpose than ourselves. We can be self-transcendent at any time, in any situation, as long as our sense of purpose is triggered. We can also be self-indulgent, selfish, and self-referenced, while ignoring our higher sense of purpose. When we're reacting to needs, we're self-referenced; when we're acting in the interests of others, groups or individuals, we're self-transcendent. And it's all unconscious until we make ourselves aware, and until we learn to balance needs satisfaction with self-transcendence.

So what, exactly, is self-transcendence, how does Core Purpose fit into this picture, and what does it mean for you?

If you're religious, you can think of self-transcendence as love. God instilled the capacity for love in us, and made it the principle characteristic of goodness, with associated ideas such as compassion, forgiveness, sacrifice, generosity, and gratitude, all of which are focused on others rather than the self. On the other hand, if you're scientifically minded, you can think of self-transcendence as an important survival trait, maybe the most important survival trait, because the social nature of humanity, more than any other characteristic, enables mankind to survive and thrive as does no other creature. Personally, I don't care about its origins. The capacity for self-transcendence exists within us, it's inborn, probably embedded in our DNA. It gives us a way to succeed in the world for our own, personal, benefit as well as the benefit of others, be they individuals, groups, or all of humanity.

Self-transcendence is not so much a need as it is a sense of purpose. The difference is important because you *react* to your needs by responding, usually unconsciously, to the urges they generate. Reacting to needs is self-referenced, selfish if you like. There's nothing wrong with that, we all need to take care of ourselves and seek personal pleasures and satisfactions. But if that's all there is, then your life is hollow indeed. It's self-transcendence that brings greater meaning into your life, and improves not only your life, but the lives of others within your circle of influence.

Your self-transcendence generates goals and intentions according to a purpose greater than yourself, while your needs create urges that you're motivated to satisfy. The trick is to find balance, so that you're serving yourself while serving the "greater self."

Have you noticed that I've consistently said, "your" self-transcendence? That's no accident. While we all have an innate, inborn self-transcendence (we can't *not* have it) it takes different forms for each of us, and it plays out differently in each of our lives. And that's what this chapter is all about, discovering *your* individual form of self-transcendence.

You can't become a truly successful entrepreneur, or anything else, without bringing your self-transcendence into balance with your needs, and you can't do that unless you discover your particular form of self-transcendence, your Core Purpose. Having done that, you can consciously use that knowledge to guide your important decisions, which include decisions you make about your business and the role it plays in your life. It's important for your happiness and sense of achievement that the work you do in your business is somehow connected to your Core Purpose.

How to Discover Your Core Purpose

Your Core Purpose isn't always easy to identify (mine wasn't) because it's usually an unconscious drive that gets formed in your developmental years. Some people discover theirs immediately, others struggle to find theirs.

It's often helpful to look at Core Purpose as the answer to three questions:

1. What impact do I want to have in the world?
2. What's right for me to do, and what's wrong?
3. What kind of person do I want to be?

Core Purpose is most easily discovered in conversation with an experienced advisor or coach, but there is an abbreviated process you can use by yourself to get some understanding of your Core Purpose.

A Process for Identifying Your Core Purpose

1. Look to your own past and identify those experiences that were meaningful or important to you. "Meaningful" doesn't mean happiness, joy, pride, or admiration from others, although those might have been part of the experience. "Meaningful" means that you found the experience deeply satisfying and derived a sense of meaningful accomplishment or contribution from the experience. The experience might be something you did, or could be something that impressed you deeply from some other source, such as a book, movie, or an event you witnessed. The only rule is that it must have been deeply meaningful to you. Make a list of as many of those experiences as you can remember.

2. Choose one experience from your list that was especially meaningful to you.

3. Mentally re-live that experience in as much detail as possible. Use the 8-sense re-experience technique to put you in touch with your unconscious mind.

4. Focus on what was meaningful about the experience. Emotions are an important guide. The stronger emotions associated with satisfaction and meaning are clues to Core Purpose. You have to "dig deep" within yourself, so don't be satisfied with your first impression of the experience. Identify as specifically as you can what was meaningful. The repeating question technique will help you drill down to what's true for you. Write down some key words to describe it.

5. Select another meaningful experience and repeat the process (steps 3 and 4). You should review at least five experiences; ten would be better, more would be better yet. One or two experiences don't reveal a pattern, and it's the pattern that will lead you to your Core Purpose. Keep your notes on separate sheets for each experience.

6. When you have re-lived your meaningful experiences, lay out all of your note sheets and look for the patterns. There's no formula for this. It's completely subjective, and you are the only person

qualified to do it because you are the only one capable of knowing what's meaningful for you.

7. Write a short statement, beginning with, "My Core Purpose is ..."

8. If you seem to have more than one possible Core Purpose, write statements for each one, and then compare them, observing your inner reactions carefully. One statement will have more emotional weight than the other(s), and that statement will lead you to your Core Purpose. Or you might find an even deeper sense of meaning that underlies both statements.

9. Condense the idea of your Core Purpose into a word or short phrase but no more than a short sentence. The phrase might be meaningless or silly to others, but it should trigger the full sense of Core Purpose in your own mind. I once had a great friend whose Core Purpose was contained in the statement, "Life is a chair of bowlies," which was a play on the old saying, "Life is a bowl of cherries." Yes, it sounds frivolous to you and me, but it was exactly right, and deeply meaningful to her. Remember, you don't have to share your Core Purpose with anyone else, but you absolutely *must* discover it for yourself. If your statement sounds silly, so what?

The central idea is to make your Core Purpose conscious so it can guide your decisions and actions in life and business. One practical way to do that is to use the three questions mentioned earlier, and apply them to important decisions in your life, while keeping your Core Purpose in your conscious awareness:

1. Will [the decision or action] result in the impact I want to have?
2. Is [the decision or action] the right thing to do?
3. Does [the decision or action] reflect the kind of person I want to be?

Money is interesting because it can be central to all of the lower level needs, and it can be a tool for serving your Core Purpose. Money buys you food, shelter, etc. and is key to satisfying survival needs. It also buys you protection and safety from threats, and the accumulation of wealth provides a great sense of security. Money also buys you access to, and makes you more welcome in many social settings and groups. It is a scorecard with which you can measure esteem needs like competence, status, and achievement, and some of your self-actualization (be all you can be) needs. Money never satisfies the need, but is a tool that can be useful at all levels of need. The accumulation of money and wealth is never Core Purpose, although it can be an important tool, self-esteem is never Core Purpose, although it can be a satisfying by-product, social acceptance, love, and belonging are not Core Purpose, although they are also desirable and satisfying in their own right, and of course, as necessary as they are, survival and security are not Core Purpose.

Here's the problem: Core Purpose is your way of reaching greater meaning and making a significant contribution. It's your response to the urge for self-transcendence, to the desire to make a meaningful contribution to something greater than yourself. But your other needs can overshadow your Core Purpose. Not only that, but some needs can masquerade as Core Purpose, especially the social and esteem needs.

So, you must be sure that the Core Purpose you discover is true self-transcendence, and not a lower level need that you mistake for Core Purpose. That's why it's important to use the repeating question to dig below the needs that might, at the moment, be driving your motivation.

Here's an example:

Caroline, a business coach trainee, had identified her Core Purpose as the following: To become the preeminent business coach in the nation. It sounded grand. Certainly the nation's preeminent business coach would be in a position to bring greater meaning and make a major contribution.

Caroline's trainer, Fred (an experienced business coach who was mentoring new coaches) suspected that Caroline was on the right track, but was being misled by her lower level needs. The following (abbreviated) conversation got Caroline to her true Core Purpose.

Fred: *Let's test your Core Purpose to be sure it's right. What is it about "becoming the nation's preeminent business coach" that's important to you?*

Caroline: Well, it would mean that I would be helping business people have better lives, and the better I did it, the better their lives would be and the more respect I'd get for making it happen.

Fred: So the respect part is what's most important?

Caroline: Well, sure, the respect part would be good, but the part that would be really meaningful would be knowing that I had improved so many lives. Having a great reputation would feel good, and status is very important to me, but more importantly, it would bring more people to me so I could help them.

Fred: So it's the "helping people have better lives" part that's the most important thing?

Caroline: Yes. I want the status, but it would be hollow if that's all there was.

Fred: What about the business people part? You only want to improve the lives of business people?

Caroline: Well, no, but that's all I know. My expertise is in business and coaching, so that's the most realistic path for me.

Fred: So, "improving peoples' lives" is the core of it, isn't it? And you focus on business people because that's where you believe you can be most effective?

Caroline: Exactly.

Fred: It sounds to me like your Core Purpose is rich, but simple: to improve people's lives. You may do it in the arena of business because that's where your skill set lies, but in your heart of hearts you seem to want to help make peoples' lives better, *and the more people you can impact, whether they're business people or not, the better.*

Caroline: *Yeah. Y'know, you're right! [Caroline's eyes opened wide at this point and she became more animated.]*

Fred: *Now, don't let me put words in your mouth. Look inside yourself. Does it feel right for you to say "My Core Purpose is to make peoples' lives better"?*

Caroline: *My Core Purpose is to make peoples' lives better. [Pauses] That's it! It makes sense and I don't have any of those little intuitive signals that happen when something isn't right for me.*

What's the point about the various levels of needs and Core Purpose? The point is that when you're identifying yours, don't be mislead by the lower level needs. Stay focused on your highest sense of purpose, and use the repeating question technique to dig deeply within yourself until you have the solid sense that you've found it.

A word of caution for you skeptics (including me before I got wise to my own Core Purpose): Core Purpose is no airy-fairy, new age, head-trip. It's a true source of motivation and commitment. It's what makes your work a joy rather than drudgery. When what you do serves your inner sense of purpose, you do it well, with energy, commitment, and power. So, please don't look at Core Purpose as simply another "power of positive thinking" gimmick. It's a real source of strength and motivation for you (and me). I hope you'll take full advantage of the power it can release in you.

CHAPTER 6

Strategic Thinking

The Key to Entrepreneur's Mind

What Is Strategic Thinking?

Strategic thinking is the ability to formulate a vision, a mental picture of what is to be achieved, and to articulate it clearly in words and images. It includes the ability to identify opportunities and alternatives, and to understand the need for change or the need not to change. It further includes the ability to see the big picture and devise an effective strategy that will lead to the realization of the vision. Finally, strategic thinking includes the ability to see beyond habitual rules and conventional wisdom, and to discover new principles, rules, and ways of behaving.

Strategic thinking comes with practice; we're all born with the aptitude, but if we don't put it to use, we never develop it. Strategic thinking also requires fuel because it feeds on information. The best strategic thinking is focused and targeted on a purpose. In fact, the first task of strategic thinking is to establish a purpose. The rest of strategic thinking is figuring out how to accomplish that purpose.

There are five habits of mind that set good strategic thinkers apart from and a quantum leap ahead of everyone else: holism, whole mind thinking, innovation, double vision, and curiosity.

Holism

Strategic thinkers see a business (or anything else) holistically, as an organism, not a collection of parts. A business is an integrated whole, not an assembly of marketing, finance, human resources, and other parts, in the same way that you are human, and not an assembly of lungs, legs, teeth, and fingers. Yes, you can look at a business or a person as a collection of parts, but when you do, you cut yourself off from truly understanding what it is to be a business or what it is to be a human.

Strategic thinkers see and understand the connectedness, the interdependence, the integrated nature of their businesses. When they consider a problem in one part of the business, they also consider the impact of that problem on everything else in the business. When they create a marketing strategy, or take out a large loan, or hire a key employee, or develop a new production system, they are aware of how each of those decisions affects the rest of the business and its customers.

The holistic view of business and life is something that most people never "get." They live their lives in a sea of disconnected, isolated parts, and have little understanding of how people and things interconnect, interrelate, and are interdependent; that's because they rarely have to.

Entrepreneurs, however, have to deal with everything in the business and everything that has an impact on the business. One moment they deal with marketing, the next an employee problem, and an instant later a production problem, all the while keeping track of customers and competition. Their world forces them to see all the different aspects of their businesses, and even the worst of business leaders eventually connect some of the dots and develop some degree of holistic thinking.

The best business leaders develop an instinct, an effective habit of mind, which enables them to integrate their thinking so that, whatever they're doing at the moment, they're always aware of the entire integrated organism that is their business.

Whole Mind Thinking

Whole mind thinking is the intentional use of both analytical thinking, which is mostly conscious and logical, and intuitive thinking, which is mostly unconscious. Most of us rely predominantly on one or the other way of thinking, analytical or intuitive. We would describe it to others with statements like, "I trust the facts," or "I trust my gut."

The importance of whole mind thinking is that the whole mind is better at decision-making. Decisions made with whole mind thinking are far more likely to be good decisions than decisions made with only one or the other way of thinking. Also, whole mind thinking, especially intuitive thinking, helps you "think outside the box," increases your creativity, and enhances your ability to see new ways of doing things, and new things to do.

Whole mind thinking increases the scope of your thought processes and opens you up to a much broader range of possibilities, opportunities, threats, challenges, and more ways to take action.

Creativity

Are you creative? If you said "no" you're wrong. You are creative; we all are. We don't all make good use of our creative potential, but we all have it. I told you this in the chapter on barriers to entrepreneurial thinking, and I'm telling you again, now.

Creativity is the part of Strategic Thinking that enables you to create ideas, practices, strategies, plans, out-of-the-box thinking, business models, new processes – any thing new or different from past habits and conventional thinking. It's also the part that opens you up to understanding other points of view, seeing all the possibilities in a situation, and generating a broader perspective of the world.

Creativity isn't constrained to the known and familiar. Conventional thinking and old habits mean nothing to your unconscious mind, and that's where creativity lives. Your unconscious mind is free-ranging and naturally creative, unless you do something to restrain it. What is something that could restrain your natural creativity? Refer back to the habits of thinking and being that I described in the earlier chapters of this book. As you continue to do the work of identifying and converting your ineffective habits of mind, your creativity will naturally re-assert itself, and you'll find yourself effortlessly thinking outside of the box. You don't have to create creativity, all you have to do is set it free, and you're already doing that if you're working on your habits of mind.

There's a grander, larger-scale form of creativity that's central to successful entrepreneurial thinking. I call it "strategic innovation" to differentiate it from the simple creativity that's released when you get your dysfunctional habits of mind out of the way. It relies on the simple creativity that effective habits of mind set free in you, but there's more to it. It's critically important for entrepreneurial thinking, so I've devoted a separate chapter to it, which you'll see later.

Double Vision

A business leader, or any leader for that matter, needs to see things from many points of view. Double vision keeps you from getting too narrowly focused and from getting entrenched into a single point of view.

There are two reasons that double vision is so valuable. One is that it enables you to pay attention to both the strategic path of your business and at the same time attend to the details of its day-to-day operation. Too many business leaders get immersed in the daily operation of the business and neglect to "come up for air" and pay attention to the strategic goals and directions that really define the future of the business. The other reason is that double vision helps keep you grounded in reality. Leadership that's removed from the reality of a situation, in other words leadership that's based on a distorted or too-narrow understanding of the situation, won't be nearly as effective as reality-based leadership.

Examples of Double Vision

Long-term	Short-term
Entrepreneurial	Operational
People as assets	People as individuals
Business viewpoint	Customer viewpoint
Strategic thinking	Operational details
Cost	Value
Intuitive	Logical
Effective	Ethical
Top down	Bottom up
Your business	Your life

For instance, one form of double vision is short-term (immediate) and long-term (future) thinking. If your attention is glued to the daily demands of the business, you can easily lose track of the big picture and stray from the strategy that will get you to your goals. On the other hand, if you don't take care of the short-term needs of your customers and your business, there will be no long-term future. Effective leaders take care of the immediate demands of the business in ways that make sure their decisions are in harmony with the long-term strategy and goals. Reality is a mix of both points of view.

Another form of double vision is the customer point of view and the business point of view. You need to keep the customer's point of view in mind in order to keep customers happy and generate a strong revenue stream, and at the same time you need to attend to the business, keeping employees productive and content, while also keeping costs down. Reality is a mix of both points of view.

Curiosity and a Hunger For Information

Strategic Thinking feeds on information. The best leaders are information junkies. It's one of the ways they stay alert for and aware of the flow of possibilities and opportunities available to their businesses. They gather information internally from their businesses and externally from all kinds of sources about all kinds of things that do or could affect the future of their businesses. They notice anything and everything that has, or might have, anything to do with their businesses. In terms of mind/ brain science, curiosity feeds your WYSIATI, and packs your unconscious thinking with the ammunition your coherence function needs to feed your conscious thinking with a more complete understanding of, well, anything.

Developing Your Strategic Thinking

People who develop their strategic thinking usually do it by living it, and responding to the pressures of business and life. It takes time because you're developing the new habits of mind that support strategic thinking. It takes time, and some trial and error, but you can accelerate the process. You can ramp up your strategic thinking quickly, with fewer of the mistakes that come with trial and error using the "key question" method.

\	\
Developing Your Strategic Thinking For important decisions, plans, and goals, use these Key Questions to stimulate and develop the five habits of strategic thinking.	
HABIT OF THINKING	**KEY QUESTIONS TO DEVELOP THE HABIT**
HOLISTIC THINKING	How does it all work together? ...**or**... Who will this decision or action affect, and how will it affect them?
WHOLE MIND THINKING	Does this make sense? ...**and**... What's my "gut feeling" about this?
CREATIVITY	What are other possibilities, even if they're unlikely or unworkable? [For important innovation, use the Innovation Process, described in the next chapter]
DOUBLE VISION	Is there another way to look at this situation or another point of view I should under- stand? ...**or**... How would others see this situation?
CURIOSITY	What's the truth, the whole truth, and noth- ing but the truth about this situation? ...**or**... What do I not know about this situation?

Ask yourself these questions every time you have an important issue, decision, plan, etc. to consider. With practice this process will become an unconscious, automatic, highly productive habit of mind.

CHAPTER 7

Strategic Innovation

Creativity with Entrepreneurial Goals

The Secret to Innovative Thinking

If you're going to become a true entrepreneur, it's a certainty that you're going to have to be creative now and then, and in significant ways. If you're one of those people who don't believe they're creative, then drop that belief like a hot potato. I've said it before in this book and I'll say it again: you are creative, you can't not be. Creativity is built into the way your brain functions and your mind works. You may not (yet) know the best ways to use your creativity, or you may have smothered your creativity under your particular lifetime of conditioning and your collection of habits of mind, but you are creative. You can't help it.

Creativity takes many forms, and the form of most concern to an entrepreneur is what I call "strategic innovation." The techniques I'll be describing in this chapter work on all forms of creativity, but you picked up a book with the word entrepreneur in the title, so strategic innovation is where I'll focus my attention.

There are proven, time-honored ways to develop creativity, and they have to do with letting your unconscious, intuitive mind loose on a problem or a goal, then reining it in with logical thinking. There's a process for it – the Innovation Process – in which your unconscious mind, in addition to powering your intuitive thinking, also powers your creativity.

In ways we don't understand, the coherence function of your unconscious mind takes in everything you perceive and all the information you gather, and somehow generates insights and breakthroughs. You know the experience; we all do. You work on solving a problem or taking advantage of an opportunity, and you come up with all kinds of possible solutions, but somehow you know they're not quite right. So you turn your mind to other pursuits. Then, when you don't expect it, the solution suddenly pops into your mind. Your unconscious mind continued to work the problem while you were sleeping or doing other things, and when it came up with the solution, that solution suddenly appeared in your conscious mind. It's the well-known "Aha moment" that we all experience from time to time.

When you dropped the problem and turned your mind to other things, or "slept on it," you took what I call a "creative pause." By gathering information and consciously thinking about the problem or opportunity you gave your unconscious mind the ammunition it needs to stimulate its creativity, but it can also need a bit of time. The creative pause puts you in a relaxed frame of mind, with minimal stress, which frees the unconscious mind to make all the connections and associations it needs to be creative. This is critical because brain science has discovered that stressful, concentrated thinking gets in the way of creativity. It's a form of the "focus blindness" I mentioned earlier in this book.

A caution: If you fill up your mind with false information, questionable assumptions, wishful thinking, and myths about business (or anything else), your unconscious mind will treat it all as reality. Your creative mechanism will work on it just fine, but if the raw material your mind has available to it is flawed, your creativity will be consistent with those flaws rather than reality. Your creative mechanism will work great, but if you feed it bad information your mind's WYSIATI ("what you see is all there is, or better stated, what you feed your brain is all it knows) will limit what your creativity can produce. The product of your creativity will be only as good as the information in your mind that it draws upon. It's the human form of GIGO: garbage in, garbage out. That's one of the main reasons I had you working on your habits of mind earlier in this book, so that your conscious and unconscious thinking will be based on reality (facts) or when facts are missing or questionable, based on reasonable assumptions, or even on the very valuable frame of mind, "I don't know." Remember, "I don't know" is a hell of a lot better than false knowledge and flawed assumptions.

So the key practice for effective innovation is first to do the information gathering and all the conscious thinking you can about the problem or opportunity, and then drop it, and turn your conscious mind to other things. Give your unconscious mind the creative pause it needs to come up with the answer to the problem, the way to take advantage of the opportunity, or the innovation you want.

A Process for Thinking Innovatively

Let me tell you a personal story about innovation. Two decades ago, when I worked for Michael Gerber, creating his E-Myth Mastery Program for him, I was intimidated by the challenge of inventing and writing more than one hundred coaching booklets of ten to forty pages each. I still remember clearly the moment I took the first booklet I wrote to Michael for his approval, thinking to myself, "Did I get it right?" My relief was enormous when he not only liked it, but was delighted that it was both innovative and true to his E-Myth principles. My relief was short-lived. Having broken the ice with the first booklet, my next thought was, "How in the world am I going to create 100 more of them?" Each booklet had to be innovative; something no other coaching business had. Yet each booklet had to be true to the E-Myth principles, usable by any business coach working with any small business leader, in any industry, and in any country. I had gotten the first one right, almost by accident as I remember. I had to come up with a systematic way to do it again, 100 times.

Well, I did it.

Long story short: I came up with an early version of the innovation process shown below. It worked. Every time. Yes, *every* time. After completing two or three more great booklets using this process, my confidence soared. By the time I completed another couple of booklets, the process had become habitual, and I knew beyond a doubt that I could, without fail, every time, produce 100 or 1,000 or any number of booklets. And later, in business and in life, when the need for innovation arose, I had a built-in habit of thinking that served me well over the years, and is still serving me well.

Like all habits, the habit of thinking innovatively is built with repetition; it takes time and practice. Use the process outlined below, and stick with it. Sooner, rather than later, it becomes habitual.

The Strategic Innovation Process

1. Clearly state the issue, problem, opportunity, or innovation you want to solve. Be clear about this because clarity will focus both your conscious and unconscious thinking. Sometimes the hardest thing to do is to state the problem, opportunity, or objective.
2. Gather and study as much information as possible about the issue. Be clear about the information you gather; know what's factual, what's questionable, and what is unknown. If you include assumptions, conventional wisdom, or questionable "facts" be aware of them. If you simply do not know some things, either leave them unknown, or if you absolutely have to, make reasonable assumptions. (Remember, what I see as a reasonable assumption, you might see as a stupid belief or vice versa.)
3. Try consciously to come up with a solution or to resolve the issue consciously and with whole mind thinking. Ask others what they think. Work at it. Do the research. Study the problem and turn over every stone in your search for the answer. Use brainstorming, guided fantasies, free association and any other techniques you know about for stimulating creativity. Exhaust all the possibilities.
4. Then take a break. Take a <u>creative pause</u> to allow your unconscious mind to continue to work on the issue. Do something completely unrelated to the problem, maybe something fun or relaxing. Sleep on it if necessary.

    This can be the most difficult part of the process, especially if you're a decisive, action-oriented person, as entrepreneurs usually are. When you don't know what's happening during this pause, it can feel lazy or irresponsible. After all, isn't "work" the answer to all your problems in business?

5. Allow the solution to emerge. You have to allow the unconscious mind to work at its own pace. If you "push it" or try too hard you disrupt and delay the unconscious process and create stress blindness.

6. When the solution, or the "aha" moment gives you an idea, you may still have to put your conscious mind to reshaping it into a workable idea. Often, the answer comes in the form of an idea or impression (that's how the unconscious mind communicates with the conscious mind), and you have to put shape and practicality to it. Remember that the conscious mind is the safeguard against the (sometimes) weirdness of the unconscious mind. The conscious mind should, in matters of importance, always be the decision-maker

Most of the time this process will result in an innovation or the best possible solution to a problem or opportunity. Now and then you'll resolve the issue while consciously working on it; you consciously arrive at the best solution or your unconscious mind works quickly. Occasionally, you never do arrive at a workable resolution as there may not *be* one.

You want this form of creativity to become habitual, but not in the same way as your other unconscious habits of mind. It shouldn't "go unconscious" in the way that you want other habits of mind to become unconscious. It's important to first do the conscious work, then let the unconscious mind do its thing, and finally finish it up with conscious thinking again to translate it all into real world action.

CHAPTER 8

Commitment

Get the Job Done, No Matter What

Where Does Commitment Come From?

Commitment is the determination, dedication, and energy to turn your entrepreneurial dream into reality, and to make your strategy succeed in the face of obstacles, opposition, uncertainty, and risk. Commitment arises from your deepest values and motivations. The strongest leaders are those whose commitment to achieving their purpose is based in deep convictions and desires. Commitment is most critical when conditions are at their worst and opposition is strongest, for that's when weak leaders fail and effective leaders persist, not stupidly or stubbornly, but with right action.

True, rock-solid commitment is a rare thing – the soldier who gives his life to achieve an objective or to save the life of a friend, the mother protecting her children, the doctor risking death from a deadly infectious disease to tend to the sick, or the entrepreneur who maxes out his credit cards, takes out a second and third mortgage on his house, cashes in his savings and retirement fund, and pours his heart and soul into his business.

Most of us only think we're committed, but when the going gets rough, or something else looks better, we shift to a different "commitment."

Where does true commitment come from? How can you harness it in yourself and use it to channel your success?

Part of the answer is Core Purpose. When you establish goals that are in harmony with and contribute to the satisfaction of your Core Purpose, you find that your commitment and your passion are hooked into your goals. When the strategy and goals of your business are in harmony with your Core Purpose, you'll find your motivation, passion, and *commitment* fully engaged and supporting everything you do.

In the final analysis, for you to be truly committed to a purpose, that purpose has to connect with your deeper values and desires, and those values and desires have to be more important to you than your own self-interest, they have to be self-transcendent.

That's why I advise you to look at your business from the perspective that it's part of your life, and to understand how a successful business contributes to a successful, gratifying life. That's why our best coaches ask their clients to identify their Core Purpose early in the coach-client relationship. Business success and financial income alone are motivating to many people, but the strongest, most enduring motivation comes from seeing the connection of your business to your life and to your deepest values and desires.

What About Obstacles, Opposition, Uncertainty, and Risk?

True commitment stands up to obstacles, opposition, uncertainty, and risk. In business, effective leaders know they'll encounter obstacles, and also know they'll overcome the obstacles. It's not that they're naïve and unrealistic about it. It's simply that they view obstacles not as barriers, but simply as conditions to be dealt with in the normal course of events.

Opposition doesn't shake the dedication of an effective leader, but is simply another condition to be dealt with and another source of information to be considered. The leader has to be realistic. Sometimes (less often than most of us think, but sometimes) the obstacle really is an insurmountable one, and sometimes the opposition really is right. Right thinking and healthy habits of mind are the capability that balances the leader and prevents commitment from becoming stubbornness.

Uncertainty doesn't shake a committed leader. The passage of time changes all things from uncertain to certain as they move from future to past, and an effective leader, grounded in reality, simply makes the best decision he can when decisions need to be made, adjusts later if need be when the actual situation materializes, and moves on toward his goals.

And of course, effective leaders have a healthy, risk-accepting (not risk-seeking) attitude, in which they see risk as a normal part of progress.

Purpose Before Self

One more thing: commitment to self. There's nothing wrong with having a large ego and being concerned about your own welfare, recognition, and success. We all have our own egos and self-concerns and they're healthy parts of any personality. You get into trouble as a leader, however, when you put yourself ahead of your purpose.

Commitment to yourself must be subordinate to commitment to purpose. We have all seen leaders whose primary purpose seems to be self-promotion. Many politicians and corporate "climbers" come to mind, and we view them with contempt, don't we? There's nothing wrong with big egos and self-promotion, they're common among successful entrepreneurs, but they must be secondary to purpose.

Testing Your Commitment to Your Business: Are You *Really* Committed?

You can test the depth of your commitment to purpose by thinking deeply about three questions:

Is your business vision aligned with your Core Purpose, or does it contribute in significant ways to your Core Purpose?

Is your business vision a powerful motivator for you?

Does your commitment to purpose have a higher priority than your commitment to yourself?

Here is some guidance for each of these questions:

Is your business vision aligned with your Core Purpose?

When your commitment is strong and aligned with your Core Purpose, you'll be self-motivated, or as is popular in today's vocabulary, you'll be "passionate" about what you're doing to accomplish your purpose. To evaluate the alignment between your Core Purpose and your business, do the following:

1. Review and confirm your Core Purpose.
2. Review and confirm your vision for your business or your "entre-preneur's dream."
3. Ask yourself, "Does my vision for my business support my Core Purpose, or at the very least are they compatible (no conflicts or inconsistencies)?"
   a. If your business vision fully supports your Core Purpose, no adjustment is needed.
   b. If your business vision is compatible (no conflicts), can it be modified to more strongly support your Core Purpose without ill effects on the business?
   c. If your business vision is inconsistent or in conflict with your Core Purpose, can it be modified to eliminate the inconsistency or conflict? Can you shift your own point of view such that your business can be seen as supportive of your Core Purpose? For instance, if you have no passion for your business, can you see it as the economic tool that enables you to pursue your Core Purpose?
   d. If you cannot resolve inconsistencies and conflicts between your business and your Core Purpose, you need to give serious consideration to the possibility that you should pursue another line of business, or some other career, one that supports your Core Purpose.

Is your business vision a powerful motivator for you?

Your business vision should be a powerful motivator for your business leadership. If it is, it'll support your commitment and your ability to influence others. If it's not, your commitment and your communications will be diminished, your leadership will be weakened, and your entrepreneurial thinking will be compromised.

Motivation and a sense of "aliveness" are powerfully affected by your emotional responses. The stronger the positive emotions associated with the achievement of your entrepreneurial dream, the stronger will be your commitment and your communications, and therefore the more effective your leadership.

The way to attach greater commitment and motivation to the achievement of your business vision is to **create associations** between strong, positive emotions and the achievement of your vision. You can do that by creating a "**success scenario.**"

A success scenario is a visualization, an 8-sense <u>pre</u>-experience, of the moment in the future when you have achieved your business vision. It's important in this visualization to focus on and even exaggerate the emotional impact you expect to experience. Emotions are important motivators. As you have seen, they can distort your thinking, but their greatest value is their ability to motivate. In this case, emotions are good because they make the visualization seem more real, and they energize you and help anchor your commitment to succeed deeply within you.

For this success scenario visualization, you should take a quiet time of about 15 minutes (more if you have the attention span) and imagine the full, 8-sense experience you expect to have when you realize that your business has succeeded. Pay special attention to, and actually feel, as much as you are able, the emotions you will feel at that time. Bring forth those emotions as powerfully as you can; experience them in your imagination. It may help to think about times in your life when you have powerfully felt those emotions in other experiences, and while retaining the feeling of those emotions, shift your thoughts back to your success scenario. That will create an association between the powerful emotion and the success scenario. Imagine and internally pre-experience strong, positive emotions such as pride, deep satisfaction, excitement, acceptance and love directed at you, a sense of accomplishment, a deep connection with your Core Purpose and the emotions associated with that, a strong sense of community with the people in your business, and any other powerful feelings and emotions that you expect success to generate in you.

Briefly write a description of your success scenario. It doesn't have to be detailed, as long as it helps you stimulate the emotions of your pre-experience whenever you recall it.

Your success scenario is a tool to help you maintain a high level of passion and motivation for your business and the way you lead it. As you're building your business, you may occasionally run into moments of discouragement or doubt. You can refer to your written statement and pre-experience your future success whenever your motivation needs a boost.

Does your commitment to purpose have a higher priority than your commitment to yourself?

What's more important to you, looking good, getting wealthy, being admired, achieving status, avoiding problems…or accomplishing your purpose? The best leaders are intensely focused on getting results and achieving their goals. They're self-interested – they want status, wealth, and a great life style – but they put their self-interests a notch or two below their purpose. They know that if they achieve their purpose, they'll get their self-interests satisfied, but they're more motivated by results than self-interest.

It's the hallmark of the best leaders: purpose before self.

There's no process to this step, however, there is a very great need for complete honesty on your part about your motivations. If you can honestly say that your primary focus is the accomplishment of your business vision, that's a strong indication that your commitment to purpose is healthy.

What about commitments to family, to country, to community, to integrity? Aren't they legitimately more important than your commitment to your business? That depends on you and your individual set of values, but that's not what's at stake here. The comparison is between commitment to purpose and commitment to self, and the more the balance weighs toward commitment to purpose, the greater will be your effectiveness.

Only you know for sure where your commitment lies on the spectrum from self to purpose. Think about it. Be completely honest with yourself. Then circle the appropriate X on the line below to show where your commitment lies.

COMMITMENT TO PURPOSE	**BALANCED COMMITMENT**	**COMMITMENT TO SELF**

If Your X is anywhere to the right of center, your commitment is in question. Most of the time it's no problem, however when times are difficult, or when there is a choice between satisfying your desires or getting results for the business, your leadership may falter.

The way to genuinely achieve an effective balance, and get your X over toward the left side of the line, is to understand, to truly realize, that the way to satisfy your desires is to put the business first and yourself second.

When you can honestly do that, you'll be on the way to genuine commitment to purpose.

CHAPTER 9

The Top Ten Business Development Principles
Shaping the Entrepreneurial Mind

There are *business* principles and there are *business development* principles, and you need to know the difference. Business principles are the underlying "laws of nature" that govern the way businesses function. They're comparable to the laws of physics or mathematics in the sciences because they're the underlying fundamentals of the way things work. You'll see them later, when I talk about the systems approach to managing a business.

Business development principles are the principles that govern the creation and continuing development of a business. They're entrepreneurial principles, and they're fundamental to business leadership. If you integrate them into your thinking, you'll be well on the road to true entrepreneurship.

The Top Ten Principles of Entrepreneurial Thinking

- #1 Put the Customer First
- #2 Systemize the Business
- #3 Deliver Full Spectrum Value
- #4 Leverage Yourself and Your Resources (the 80/20 Rule)
- #5 Apply Principles, Not Formulas
- #6 Quantify (But Don't Overdo It)
- #7 Define Success
- #8 Focus on Results
- #9 Keep Your "SWOT" Turned On
- #10 Keep a Healthy Perspective

Let's start with a simple definition of a business. I use this definition to establish several key principles and to keep focused on what's most important and will result in a successful business.

A business is a system for delivering value to customers

This definition of a business leads us to the first three business development principles, which are indicated by the words "customer," "system," and "value." First and foremost of these entrepreneurial principles is:

Principle #1: Put the Customer First

The customer must be paramount. Of all the people interested in your business, by far the most important are customers. You might be tempted to think of yourself or your investors or your employees as the most important, but they and you are all secondary. In truth they might actually be primary, but unless you serve your customers and fully satisfy their needs, no one else's needs get served. So, even if you don't really believe your customers are more important than yourself or your investors, treat them like they're the *only* important people in the world. If you don't satisfy your customers, it's all a waste of time. Your business won't survive, and nobody gets satisfied.

The customer is *everything* for a business. Don't ever forget it, not for a moment.

Principle #2: Systemize the Business

A business is a system of systems within systems. That may sound like gobbledygook, but it's not. Systems are the foundation of business excellence and the best way to find simplicity within complexity.

Systemizing your business is the surest way to get the reliable, consistent, high quality, and cost-effective results that are necessary for success, so transforming your business from a struggling, failing business into a successful one is a process of creating and managing effective business systems.

I talk a lot about systems because they're the primary tool for building a business that delivers value for everyone.

Speaking of value...

Principle #3: Deliver Full Spectrum Value

Value is one of those words that means what you think it means, depending on your point of view. In business, value is anything you provide that someone wants. If you provide it but they don't want it, it's valueless. If they want it but don't get it, it's valueless. If they want it and get *all* of it, that's full spectrum value.

There's a basic mistake many business people make about value. They think mainly in economic terms that value means money or anything that can be measured by money. That's wrong. Well, it's not really wrong, it's just narrow and shortsighted. Economic value is extremely important, essential, actually, but there's much more to it.

To the owner value is wealth, profits, satisfaction, making a contribution, status and more. To customers value is a good price for the products and services they buy, a good experience with the product and the provider they get it from, status, emotional satisfaction and more. To an employee value is a paycheck, job satisfaction, a good working environment, respectful treatment and more. To the community value is a business that pays its taxes, provides jobs for its citizens, contributes to the positive energy and the economics of its community and more.

Think of value this way: There's economic value which is measured by money and there's "full spectrum" value, which means anything that satisfies needs, including money. For instance, people buy automobiles for transportation, status, a fun experience, self-image, emotional impulses, and, yes, also for economic reasons, and people buy candy bars for flavor, to ease hunger, for emotional comfort, or possibly other reasons.

A successful business provides a full spectrum of value to its customers. And don't forget that value is in the eye of the beholder; value is what **they** say it is, not what **you** say it is. You may think you offer the best products and services since sliced bread, but if nobody is buying, those great products and services are worthless.

Principle #4: Leverage Yourself and Your Resources (the 80%-20% Rule)

Effective people know to focus their attention and their resources on the small number of tasks that get the greatest results. The trick is in knowing *which* work and resources will get the results they want. It's called the eighty-twenty rule because typically, in any endeavor, about eighty percent of the results produced by a person or a business are produced by about twenty percent of the work.

What are the driving forces in the business? That's where you put your attention. What elements of value drive the customer's purchase decision? That's where you put your attention. What systems in the business are the ones that get the most important results? That's where you put your attention. What are the highest priorities for work to be done? That's where, well, you know.

Principle #4 asks you to figure out what "drives" your business, what "drives" your customers, what "drives" your employees, and to focus your attention on those drivers.

Principle #5: Apply Principles Not Formulas

When I say "formula" I include rules, templates, best practices, and other "cookie cutter" methods, which are simply attempts to transplant methods that worked in one business into other businesses.

Formulas make sense, don't they? If a rule works for one business shouldn't it work for any business, or at least any similar business? If a template succeeds in one business, shouldn't it work for another? If a best practice is proven, shouldn't you use it?

The problem with formulas is not that they don't work, they're popular because they do work. They're relatively easy and you don't have to think much about them. You simply use them to imitate what others have done. And that seems to make sense. Why shouldn't you imitate a formula that works?

The problem with formulas is this: your business isn't the same as any other business (not even other businesses offering the same products and services to the same markets) and you're not like other business leaders. You have your own strengths and weaknesses, they're not like anyone else's, and your specific situation isn't exactly like the situation for any other business. So, if you use a formula approach to developing your business, it might help you make progress, but it won't be ideal for you and your business. You may even get good results, but you won't get *great* results.

Formulas can help you make progress, and if you don't know there's a better way, you'll be satisfied. But there is a better way; apply *principles* not formulas.

So what exactly does *that* mean?

A business principle is an underlying business reality. A business principle is deeper, more fundamental than a formula. A formula is a generalized attempt to solve a general business problem. But your problems (and opportunities) aren't general, they're *specific*. Specific to your business, specific to your ways of managing, specific to your markets, specific to your products, and specific to your financial situation. At best, a formula will "sort of" fit your business, and at worst, it will be counterproductive.

What you need are specific solutions to your specific problems and opportunities. You don't want "approximately" or "good enough." You want "exactly right" for your business, and "outstanding" for your customers, investors, employees, and others. So when you learn about a formula that worked for some other business, or one you find in a textbook, don't use just the formula but find the underlying business realities on which the formula is based, the business principles, and apply *those* to your business. That's what a true entrepreneur does.

Principle #6: Quantify (But Don't Overdo It)

It's hard to be objective about your business. Your me-bias alone skews your judgment, and so do your confirmation bias and your desires. And that's just the mental part. Because you're human, you react more to dramatic events than routine ones, and the dramatic or unusual will weigh more heavily in your perceptions than reality would suggest. Also, you can't see everything all at once or be everywhere at once. In other words, as a human being, with the mind of a human being, you can't easily be objective about your business. And if you can't be objective, you can't be rational.

Quantification brings rationality and reality to your perceptions. It helps your Reality B match up with the Reality A of your business.

There are two ways to quantify, and, yes, you can quantify anything, even art and emotions. The first is to measure. How many products does your business make in a day? How many customers does it serve? What does it cost to make a product, or serve a customer? Anything you can put a number to can be quantified, and once you've quantified it, you can observe it objectively, and make rational judgments about it.

In this world of ours, there are lots of things that can't be measured with a ruler or some other kind of instrument, but you can still use quantification to make rational judgments about them. It's like judging diving or gymnastics in the Olympics Games. You observe the action and give it a score, a rating of some kind. For instance, diving judges appraise each dive and score it from zero to ten, based on the qualities that define a good or bad dive. It's not as precise as measurement, but it's a *lot* more precise than trying to judge the quality of a dive without a scoring system, and it forces the judges to think rationally about the dive, compare it in their minds with the criteria for a good dive, and give it a score. And that allows them to be much more objective about their observations, and therefore rational about their judgments, and therefore fair.

You can quantify anything and everything, but don't. Over-quantification just creates information clutter and confusion. The secret to quantification (hinted at in the 80/20 rule) is to focus on the things that make a real difference in the business. Revenues, costs, profits, and the cash position of the business always make a difference, so you always quantify them. Customer satisfaction always makes a difference, so you always quantify that, usually in several different ways. Part of the entrepreneur's craft is to understand what's important and what's not, and quantify those things that make a difference.

It's critically important for an entrepreneur to have an accurate Reality B about his business, and quantification is one of the best tools for doing exactly that.

Principle #7: Define Success

It's only after the fact (after you've accomplished something) that you can call it a success. Before the fact it's a hope, or if you're smart about it, a goal. Setting goals is actually defining success before it happens. Goals give you something to aim for, something to direct your efforts, something to motivate you, and something to keep you on course.

The first point about defining success is the simple act of doing it. The mere fact that you define success before leaping into an activity goes a long way toward insuring that you will, in fact, be successful. So look ahead and consciously decide what success means to you and to your business. And yes, you need to consider two kinds of success; success for your business, and success for yourself.

What is success for you? It's what you say it is.

Well, it's not quite that simple. Yes, you should define success in a way that's meaningful for you, but be careful. Most of us define success in conventional terms such as wealth, possessions, status, acceptance from others, health, inching the other guy out across the finish line, going to the moon, getting an A in algebra, curing cancer, learning to play the guitar; anything you accomplish can be defined as a success. Stripped to the essentials, *success is nothing more than setting a goal and achieving it.*

What if the goal isn't right for you? Is it still success? Most people would say yes. If your goal is to make a million dollars by the age of twenty-five, and you do it, would anyone deny your success? If your mother and father want you to be a doctor, and you do, isn't that a success? Yes, of course, these are examples of success. But maybe not.

There's a deeper experience of success. Each of us has an inner drive that motivates us. It appeared earlier in this book where I told you about Core Purpose. It's something that's so basic that it seems inborn, an innate part of our characters. It's also something that operates mostly at an unconscious level, and it needs to become a part of our conscious awareness so we can factor it into our decision-making, and use it to tap into our passion and motivation. It's not mysterious, but most of us need a bit of thought in order to get a clear, conscious understanding of it. The main point about Core Purpose is that the goals you set for yourself and your business shouldn't conflict with your Core Purpose or you're setting yourself up for failure or an unfulfilling life and career. Making Core Purpose part of your *conscious* thinking sets you up for success.

What is success for your business? Again, success is what you say it is.

And again, it's not quite that simple. Defining success for your business should be done in a way that actually launches you toward that success. Goals, mission, and vision for the future are essential for success, according to conventional business thinking, and I agree with that. But they're not enough. Goals, vision, and mission don't get anything started. They're static, inert. Your business vision should launch you into the actual steps of achieving that future, so later in this book, I'll teach you something called "Strategic Intent." As the name implies, Strategic Intent is a clear statement of what the business will become in the future when it's successful, and the goals it will accomplish. But it's more than that because it actually puts you on the path to that future with a statement of the business model that you'll be using, the business "personality" you'll develop in your people, and how the business will be "positioned" for success.

Principle #8: Focus on Results

Everything done by you or your business has an outcome, a result. The very purpose of a business is to produce results in the form of value for anyone with an interest in the business, especially customers.

The mistake business people make is to focus on the work, not the results. The purpose of work is to produce a result. If you focus on the work, you get what you get. If you focus on the result, it will direct the work toward the outcome you want, and you'll get what you want to get. It's actually a chain of purpose:

GOALS ➜ WORK ➜ RESULTS ➜ SUCCESS

It's a simple but powerful principle: set goals to achieve the results you want and keep your eye on those results as you work toward them.

Principle #9: Keep Your "SWOT" Turned On.

First of all, what's "SWOT"? SWOT is the acronym for "strengths, weaknesses, opportunities, and threats," and SWOT analysis is a well-known technique for looking at a business to make decisions about its future. I'll go more deeply into SWOT analysis in the chapter on Strategic Action, but in a nutshell, it's this: Every business has strengths and weaknesses, things it does well or poorly, or resources that give it advantages and disadvantages in competition with other businesses and in the minds of its customers. Every business also faces threats that work against it and opportunities that it could exploit to become more successful. Strengths, weaknesses, opportunities, and threats are always in constant motion, changing continually; nothing is ever static in business.

SWOT analysis is a valuable tool for planners, and it's a useful technique to learn. More importantly, however – and all true entrepreneurs know this – SWOT can be a state of mind rather than a one-time analysis. True entrepreneurs have that SWOT mindset. They are constantly aware, continually updating, and always on the alert; their radars are always switched ON. They know at all times the strengths and weaknesses of their businesses. They are alert for, and therefore detect before others do, the threats that could harm their businesses, and emerging opportunities that could help them.

Principle #10: Keep a healthy perspective

Part of building a successful business is also building a successful life. This is as much a life principle as it is a business principle. The relationship between your business and the rest of your life – your family, friends, service activities, leisure time, and even sleep time – needs to be kept in balance. For most business leaders, the business commands the lion's share of their time, attention, and even passion. No one but you can say what the right balance is, but the chances are high that you're not in balance right now. You might be the rare exception but you probably aren't.

Your business should contribute to your life, not dominate it. It should bring you quality and fulfillment, not drag you down and wear you out.

Part Three: The What, the How, and the Inner Workings of a Successful Business

CHAPTER 10

Define Success

Strategic Intent ... the "What"

The Shape of Things to Come

Principle #7 of the previous chapter is "Define Success." Most business practitioners do that with a vision and mission statement. It's common knowledge that having a clear vision and mission provide you with a sense of the future of your business and help you avoid straying off in unproductive directions. The problem with vision and mission statements is, while they point you in the right direction, they don't help you take the first step. Strategic Intent does. Strategic Intent *is* the first step toward business success; it establishes the goals, sets the path, and gets you started on the path. Strategic Intent is the shape of things to come, specifically the shape of your business in the future: it's place in the world, how it does business, its character and personality, and how it creates value.

And just as importantly, creating the Strategic Intent of your business helps develop your strategic thinking, a fundamental aspect of the entrepreneurial mind.

Strategic Intent has the following components:

Strategic Positioning refers to the place your business will occupy among all businesses. It defines the arena in which the business will operate. It answers the question, "What kind of business will it be?"

Strategic Differentiation as the name implies, focuses on what will make your business and your products different from, and better than the others that customers might choose. What characteristics (from the customers' viewpoint) will set the business apart *favorably* from other businesses with similar strategic positioning?

Business Model What will be the business's key operating systems and financial characteristics? How will it function and make a profit? How will it build value for its owners? How will it deliver value to customers?

Business Personality What key values, beliefs, and behaviors will bind the people of your business into an effective team? What is the intended personality (the character) of the business?

Strategic Goals What are the major goals you want the business to achieve, and when will they happen?

Notice there are no vision or mission statements. Why, in this day and age, when it's common knowledge that vision and mission are fundamental for any business, don't I include them? Well actually, I do, and much more.

The ideas of vision and mission are woven into Strategic Intent. In fact some business experts would tell you that Strategic Intent is nothing more than a fancy vision and mission statement; they would be wrong. Vision and mission have no action built into them, they're ideas, important ideas certainly, but just ideas. Strategic Intent requires you to think through the basic structure and character of the business, what place it occupies in the world of commerce, how it compares and contrasts with competitors, and, in broad strokes, how it will operate, deliver value to customers, and make money. Strategic Intent requires you to make some important decisions and leads you into action. That's a lot more than vision and mission do; it's strategic thinking with an action bias.

The bottom line is that Strategic Intent is really a set of business decisions you make now that guide the development and growth of your business. You may shift strategies and business plans from time to time, but the destination set by your Strategic Intent should be fairly stable and not change with the pressures of the day. It can and should change, however, when major market forces shift, key laws change, significant opportunities appear, or other important factors develop.

Strategic Positioning - What Kind of Business Will It Be?

If you were allowed only one or two sentences to describe your Strategic Intent, the answer would be your strategic positioning. It's the ten-second sound bite that tells someone the very few, most important facts about what you intend your business to achieve. Some examples:

Mike's Garage is an auto repair shop that provides all kinds of automotive repair and maintenance (except body work) within a 30-mile radius of downtown Northburg.

Selma's Beautique is a high-end, high-fashion beauty salon, offering a full range of beauty treatments to upscale customers in and around Anytown.

Tek-Tek, Inc. is a business-to-business provider of information technology services for office management in small and medium sized businesses. Tek-Tek provides needs analysis, systems design, equipment sourcing, purchase negotiation, installation, training, servicing, and aftermarket upgrading of all business hardware and software, anywhere in the San Francisco Bay Area.

MaxFit is a fitness center, providing a wide variety of strength, aerobic, and agility equipment, swimming and aquatic activities, racquet sports, health and fitness classes, and fitness-related social activities to customers of all ages on the North side of Sacramento, and soon to be franchised to other communities.

The Townville Restaurant is a family-centered restaurant serving the communities in and around Morris County, Texas, with a focus on hearty, down-home food, fast, friendly service, a fun atmosphere, and affordable prices.

Strategic Positioning identifies the name of the business, the kind of product or service offered, the general target market, and maybe an idea of competitive standing, pricing, quality, customer service or other important characteristics of the business.

If you were unable to say more than these one or two sentences, you would still have communicated the essence of what you want to achieve with your business.

Strategic Differentiation – How Will the Business Be Better Than the Others?

Unless your business is a monopoly, it'll be in competition with other businesses. Strategic differentiation is the way you plan to set your business apart from other businesses so that your business has a competitive advantage over them, in other words, *favorable* differentiation. Businesses differentiate themselves on the basis of price, quality, convenience, innovation, superior customer service, etc., and they use descriptions like better, best, leading, value, low price, unique, unsurpassed, etc. to describe their advantages.

If your elderly, uneducated uncle, who knows nothing about business, asked you, "Why's your business better?" Your answer (which you'd keep short and simple for your uncle's benefit) would be your statement of strategic differentiation.

To illustrate, here are statements of strategic differentiation for the examples shown above for strategic positioning:

Mike's Garage: We offer the best trained mechanics, using the highest quality, brand-name parts, and we provide a free 70-point inspection to insure the quality of our work, and to keep customers up to date about the "health" of their cars.

Selma's Beautique: We are the only beauty salon in the area that provides "Hollywood quality" beauty treatments and products, yet we keep our prices affordable for our customers.

Tek-Tek, Inc: We provide our customers with the unique Tek-Tek No-Surprise Work Plan, which locks in our pricing and guarantees our products and services before the customer says "yes." We can do this because our integrity and the quality of our work are the best in the business.

MaxFit: We have the best, most up-to-date fitness equipment, the cleanest and most customer-friendly facilities, fitness classes designed around our customers' needs, and an atmosphere that feels more like family than business.

The Townville Restaurant: Our family-centered restaurant feeds you the absolute best down-home comfort food anywhere, yet we keep our prices affordable for all.

Business Model – How Will the Business Operate?

A business model is an overview of how your business functions. If a stranger asked you, "How does your business work?" your answer would be your business model. You'd mention the major characteristics and key systems of the business, and you'd say something about the revenue and profit generating strategies. You wouldn't go into detail, but you would give a clear impression of what makes things tick in the business. For example, here's how the owner of a landscape services business might describe her business model:

We operate a retail garden and landscape supply store in the northern suburbs of Bigville. We do landscaping for residential and commercial construction companies in the area. We advertise on local radio and in the local press, and we have a salesperson for our commercial accounts.

We make home deliveries of plants and landscape supplies, and we offer landscape design services for a fee that we discount based on the amount of the customers purchase and past business. Our pricing is toward the upper range of comparable businesses in the area, reflecting our superior value.

We don't grow any of our plants or make any of our landscape supplies; we buy them and mark them up about 100% on average for resale. We keep large inventories because our suppliers aren't always reliable, and we don't want to run out of high-demand items.

We're more concerned with quality and customer service than efficiency. We offer no-questions, money-back guarantees on all our work and products.

As we grow our business by expanding to the southern and western suburbs, we'll be purchasing centrally and distributing to our local stores. That will give us buying power, lower our costs, and allow us to cut our prices.

The business model enables you to decide on and take the next steps toward achieving your Strategic Intent. You simply take stock of your present business model, look at the business model you'll be using when you reach your Strategic Intent, and begin the process of improving existing systems in your business and creating the new systems that will be needed.

Business Personality – The Character of the Business

Just as a person has a personality, so does a business. It's made up of the combined beliefs and behavior of all the people in the business, and can be shaped by the owner.

What kind of business personality will best contribute to the achievement of your Strategic Intent? Should your business be an aggressive, cutthroat competitor? Should it be a warm and friendly place, or should it be serious and professional? What kind of moral-ethical atmosphere

> ## Business Personality
>
> *What shapes the thinking and the behavior of the people in the business?*
>
> **Values** What's right or wrong, acceptable or unacceptable, important or unimportant?
>
> **Norms** What is normal and acceptable behavior?
>
> **Beliefs** What is accepted as true or desirable?
>
> **Attitudes** What mindset and feelings should prevail about matters of importance?

should it have? Should it "play by the rules" at all times, or should it be willing to cut corners to achieve its objectives? What do you want the people in the business to believe? The customer is always right? Profit is king?

What kind of mindset do you want to prevail in the business? Is it okay to take the initiative and take a risk, or do you have to follow the rules no matter what? Get the sale whatever it takes, or do what's best for the customer? Fear the boss, or see him/her as an ally? Family first, or work first?

You can see that some kinds of business personalities help the business, while others might hinder it. Your Strategic Intent should reflect a business personality that "fits" the kind of business you want to create and supports its goals. A "take it slow" mentality won't work for a business in an aggressive, fast-changing industry. On the other hand, a fast-changing business personality won't work for customers who value stability and long-term results.

Strategic Goals - Track Your Progress

Strategic Intent is itself a major goal. It's what you want your business to achieve at a future point in time. How will you know you're on the right path, and how will you know when you've arrived? Your strategic goals will tell you when you've met or exceeded the goals.

> ### STRATegic Goals
>
> **S**ignificant
>
> **T**ime specific
>
> **R**ealistic yet challenging
>
> **A**ctionable and focused
>
> **T**rackable (quantifiable and observable)

Goal-setting is both an art and a science. The right goals and the right number of goals can and should keep you on the path to success and keep you motivated; the wrong goals can lead you astray.

The acronym "STRAT" will help you set effective goals by reminding you that a strategic goal should be:

Significant The goal should be an important indicator of the successful achievement of your Strategic Intent. You can set goals for minimizing telephone expenses, for instance, and that can be important for cost controls, but it's not a strategic, big-picture goal and it doesn't reflect the achievement of your Strategic Intent. On the other hand, setting a goal of, say, sales revenue of $10 million for the year 20XX is significant, and it's a key indicator of reaching the Strategic Intent.

Time-specific Set a time frame for achieving the goal: "within 5 years" or "by December 31, 20XX." Time has a habit of getting away from you unless you focus on it. Target dates and deadlines provide the focus.

Realistic, yet challenging Easy goals are boring and de-motivating and they don't inspire. They do, however, encourage laziness and underachievement. Impossible goals are de-motivating in a different way. They cause you to give up before you start. They make your people think, "It's an impossible goal, why even try?" The key to both motivation and achievement is to set goals that are difficult yet reachable, and provide rewards that make achieving the goal worth the effort. If you're new to goal setting, it may take a bit of experience to get to the point where you can set goals with just the right balance of challenge and achievability.

Actionable and focused A goal has to focus on one quantifiable or observable result, and it has to be something you can take action to achieve. The goal of "being the best in the market" isn't actionable. What is "best"? To make it actionable, you have to make it specific by defining it. For instance, "best" might mean number one in sales revenues or unit sales, it might mean the highest satisfaction ratings from customers, it might mean the largest market share, or most profitable, or any number of other results. If you focus on results, specific results, your goal will be actionable.

Trackable You must be able to track your progress toward achieving the goal, and that means there must be something you can measure or observe that tells you about your progress and when you've achieved the goal. Most results in business can be measured in some way such as dollars of revenue, units of sales, costs, quality, efficiency, and the like.

What about things that can't be measured? Things like employee morale, product style, customer satisfaction, the friendliness of a sales person, or ethical behavior, to name a few? What can't be measured can be quantified. Quantification isn't as precise as measurement, but it's a lot more objective and reliable than making no effort to quantify the non-measurable. Quantification is simply a matter of setting up a scale, say from 1 to 10, or A, B, and C, or estimating a percentage based on 100% as "perfect." Any way you can express your judgment numerically or in the form of a scale is a way to quantify a non-measurable goal.

Write Your Statement of Strategic Intent and Communicate It

Everyone in your business needs to know and understand its Strategic Intent, so you have to write it down. It has to be as brief as you can make it without losing any important ideas, and as long as it needs to be without adding any fluff. It has to be in simple language, and it can't make any unbelievable claims or demands on the business, or people won't take it seriously.

Communicate the Strategic Intent to everyone in your business so they know where the business and they are headed. Announce it in a company meeting or refer to it in your conversations with employees. Make it easily visible and frequently seen; put it on posters, in manuals, or on wallet cards given to everyone. The point is to keep people aware of the business's Strategic Intent so it becomes a part of their understanding of the business and their jobs within it.

Write Your Statement of Strategic Intent

Strategic Positioning
What kind of business do you want it to be?

Strategic Differentiation
How will the business stand out as better than the competition?

Business Model
How will the business do what it has to do, and how will it make a profit?

Business Personality
What kind of team will you need to achieve your strategic goals?

Strategic Goals
How will you know you've succeeded? When will that be?

Strategic Intent is a beacon and a magnet and without it you struggle with the uncertainties of trial and error or the vagueness of "strategic wishing." Business development is challenging enough. You don't have to make it more so by lacking a clear path to a clear future. Strategic Intent focuses you on that future and puts you on that path. It's both a beacon showing you the way and a magnet drawing you forward.

CHAPTER 11

Set Strategy

Strategic Action ... the "How"

The Driving Forces of Your Business

Strategic Intent is the "what" of business strategy. What do you intend to accomplish? Strategic Action is the "how" of business strategy. How are you going to accomplish it? The two in combination, Strategic Intent plus Strategic Action, form your business strategy.

Business Strategy = Strategic Intent + Strategic Action

Business strategy consists of managing the driving forces – the strengths and weaknesses of your business and the opportunities and threats it faces from the external world – so that the result will be success, in other words, the achievement of your Strategic Intent.

What drives your business? You do, of course. And that's the ultimate truth about small business success or failure. You, the owner, the leader, the CEO, the boss (however you think of yourself) are the primary driving force behind the business. It's a pretty awesome responsibility, but there's no reason to be intimidated by it if you understand all the other driving forces (controllable and uncontrollable) and how to deal with them.

That's the key, isn't it? Understanding all the *other* forces that influence your business and dealing with them. When you have a realistic understanding of the various forces that impact the success of your business, you can manage the controllable ones, and take advantage of or avoid the uncontrollable ones. That's the path to success, to achieving your Strategic Intent.

However, there's a problem. There are hundreds, probably thousands, of forces large and small that influence your business. How can you even identify them all, much less understand and manage them? You can't, not all of them. But you can focus on the small number of forces that have the greatest influence – the "driving" forces of your business. The key is the 80/20 Rule. Remember? In any endeavor about 20% of the resources and effort produce about 80% of the results. So when you're looking at the forces that drive your business – the uncontrollable ones as well as the controllable ones – you'll want to focus on the ones that have the biggest impact.

That leads us to the purpose of this chapter, which is to help you identify and make decisions about the forces, other than yourself, that drive your business so you can manage the controllable ones and cope with the others in productive ways.

"SWOT" Identifies the Driving Forces

There are four kinds of driving forces that shape a business and lead to its success or failure. Two of them, strengths and weaknesses, are internal to the business and are for the most part controllable by you. The other two, opportunities and threats, are external and are mostly not controllable. You have to deal with them, but you usually can't control them.

Strengths, Weaknesses, Opportunities, and Threats = SWOT

It's best to look first externally, at opportunities and threats, because that helps you judge strengths and weaknesses. How do you know something is a strength if you don't know what opportunities it will help you exploit or what threats it will help you avoid?

The best way to look at your SWOTs is to lay them out in a four-box grid, using a word or phrase to identify each strength, weakness, opportunity, or threat. Here's an example for Johnson's Landscaping, a small landscape and gardening business. Look it over to get a general idea of what SWOT is all about.

SWOT ANALYSIS JOHNSON'S LANDSCAPING	
STRENGTHS	**WEAKNESSES**
▪ Only landscaper in the local area – nearest competitor 27 miles away ▪ Excellent market awareness, very strong word of mouth ▪ In business 35 years; great reputation ▪ Experienced, high-skill maintenance and planting crews ▪ Excellent landscape designer on staff ▪ Staff has strong commitment to customers and quality of work	▪ High debt from last year's expansion; repayment will drag profits for five more years ▪ Owner approaching retirement, not able to work as much. Marketing depends on her. ▪ Availability of land-moving crews and equipment is erratic. Sometimes delays work. ▪ Plant suppliers unreliable and not many suppliers in the area
OPPORTUNITIES	**THREATS**
▪ Growing area (we're in a major suburb of Bigville, 18 miles away). Two major housing projects underway with many more planned in the ten-year future. ▪ Area is becoming more upscale, less do-it-yourself; demand for yard maintenance service and professional landscaping is increasing ▪ Cost of plants is declining so we can keep prices low	▪ Growth in the area will attract competitors. ▪ Limited water supply conditions and water restrictions beginning to cut into the landscaping business. ▪ Environmental activists opposing fertilization and pest control chemicals. Not a big deal now, but they seem to be making inroads. Might have new regulations that could diminish our business. ▪ Labor costs going up.

Opportunities are those conditions outside your business that help your business succeed. An opportunity could be a product need in your market, a weakness in a competitor, a change in the law that helps you, a new technology that will reduce your costs or provide better products or services to your customers, a change in the economic situation that helps you (like lower interest rates for your loans), easier availability of an important resource (such as cheaper telephone services, a better location for serving your market, a new machine that lowers your costs or provides higher quality service, etc.).

Threats are the opposite. They are conditions outside your business that diminish the ability of your business to succeed. Examples are the opposites of the opportunity examples just mentioned.

Opportunities and threats aren't controllable by you, they just happen. Sometimes you can influence them, but you always have to deal with them. You do that by developing your strengths and reducing or eliminating your weaknesses. And by "your" we mean your own personal strengths as well as those of your business. Often, *very* often, it's the strengths and weaknesses of the business owner or key managers that need attention as well as those of the business. So, when you do your SWOT analysis, look at yourself as an important part of the picture.

Strengths are those conditions or abilities within your business that enable you to succeed. What is it that gives you an advantage over your competitors, that puts you first in the eyes of your customers, that keeps your costs low, or that makes you an innovator in your markets? Those are strengths.

Weaknesses put you at a disadvantage. Ineffective or missing systems, high costs, poor image in your markets, products that don't work, services that don't serve, a bad location, poorly trained employees, and lack of responsiveness to customers are examples of weaknesses.

Keep the Big Picture in Mind: SWOT is Strategic, Not Operational

The whole purpose behind SWOT analysis is to know the forces that are driving your business, understand which of them are controllable and not controllable, and use that knowledge to create a strategy for reaching your Strategic Intent.

What is strategy? Essentially, the strategy consists of the answers to questions like these:

What opportunities do we want to exploit? Do we have the strengths to do so?

*What opportunities **can** we take advantage of, given our strengths and weaknesses?*

What strengths don't we have that we need?

What weaknesses will get in our way, and how can we either eliminate them or convert them to strengths?

What threats face us, and how can we cope with them? What weaknesses make us vulnerable and what can we do about that? Is there any way to turn threats into opportunities? Can we avoid the threats?

There's a lot of academic mystery about strategy, but when you get practical about it, strategy is nothing more than deciding what opportunities you want to take advantage of, what threats you want to avoid, and what systems you want to put in place to be successful. In other words, ***your strategy consists of the choices you make about opportunities, threats, strengths, and weaknesses, and the systems you decide to put in place to back up your choices.***

The bottom line about business strategy is simply this: SWOT analysis *is* your strategic planning process, and the decisions you make about your SWOTs, along with your Strategic Intent, *are* your strategic plan.

The centerpiece of your strategy is your Strategic Intent, which you learned about in the previous chapter. SWOT helps you make the decisions that will enable you to achieve your Strategic Intent. You'll often find that, as you do your SWOT analysis, you learn things that can make you re-think your Strategic Intent. Doing SWOT analysis is a way of increasing your knowledge, (the WYSIATI that your mind has to work with as it does its conscious and unconscious thinking) which in turn makes you more savvy about your strategy decisions. So, as you do your SWOT analysis, you may decide to modify your Strategic Intent.

The way to create a Strategic Intent that has the best chances for success is to do it in three steps:

First, create a "first pass" Strategic Intent. It's a picture of what you're trying to achieve with your business, and how it will look and operate when you've achieved it. It's your dream for the future. You've probably already done this.

Secondly, do a SWOT analysis. Get an in-depth, thorough understanding of the forces driving your business, and especially, get an honest, no-wishful-thinking understanding of your strengths and weaknesses, the value of opportunities, and the severity of threats.

Finally, get real. Does your Strategic Intent match up with your SWOT analysis? Do you have or can you develop the strengths needed to achieve your Strategic Intent? Are your weaknesses fixable? Do you as the leader have the skills and motivation to make it all happen? When you line up your Strategic Intent with your SWOTs, is it all do-able? If so, great. Go for it. If not, you might have to adjust your Strategic Intent. Either way, you greatly increase your prospects for success with an honest, hard-nosed SWOT.

It's best to do the SWOT analysis *after* developing your first pass at your Strategic Intent, not before. Without some idea of what you're trying to achieve you don't know what your strengths or weaknesses are. Strengths for what? Compared to what? You have to know what kind of game you're playing to know your strengths and weaknesses.

Imagine yourself, for instance, as a muscular, tall, fast athlete, with amazing reflexes. Those should all be strengths, right? But what if your chosen sport, your Strategic Intent, lies in the field of horse racing? Jockeys need great reflexes, so that would be a strength, but tall and muscular (heavy) would be weaknesses. On the other hand, you might be perfect for basketball. You might have to adjust your "Strategic Intent" to a sport for which you're better suited.

Guidelines for SWOT Analysis

Start by starting – just do it.

Start your SWOT list by thinking about the SWOT elements yourself, and discussing them with people you trust. Grab a large piece of paper, make a four-box grid, and quickly write as many SWOTs as you can think of.

Sometimes it's not clear if something is an opportunity or a strength. If you happen to have the best store location of all your competitors, or you have the best-known name in your line of business in your market area, or if you have a cost advantage that lets you underprice the competition, all these can all seem like opportunities. You have the "opportunity" to draw more customers with your great location, your best-known name, or your pricing advantages. These are all things you control, and are actually strengths. They enable you to take advantage of the opportunities in your target markets.

They key is controllability. If it's controllable, it represents a strength or weakness. If it's not controllable, it represents an opportunity or threat, and depending on your strengths and weaknesses, you may or may not be able to take advantage of the opportunity or cope with the threat.

You'll probably come up with most of your SWOTs with this quick and easy brainstorming process, but don't stop there.

Use the top ten checklist of business functions to identify strengths and weaknesses

Just as your body has to have many parts (head, torso, stomach, heart, brain, fingers, etc.), and has to successfully perform many functions (breathing, digestion, elimination, pumping your blood, muscle function, perspiration, etc.), so too does your business have to have many parts (people with many skills, and assets like rooms, furniture, machinery, information, cash, inventory, etc.), and has to perform many functions (accounting, marketing, production, customer services, cash management, communications, etc.). To help you identify and evaluate your strengths and weaknesses you can use the following list of business activities to jumpstart your thinking.

Leadership: the work that establishes strategy and business plans, builds the business culture, inspires the business's people to do their best for customers, the business, and themselves; being a creative force in the business

Systematics: working with employees to create systems for doing the work of the business; organizing the business and its systems

Supervision: the work of overseeing and mentoring the people in the business, developing them, making the best use of the people of the business, designing an effective system of rewards and discipline that taps into their motivations

Market Research: work that enables you to understand markets, select your target markets, and determine your target customer's needs

Marketing Communications: work that enables you to reach your target markets through the right channels with messages that will attract and persuade them

Sales and Customer Relationships: work that interacts directly with potential customers, converts them to actual customers, and then manages customer relationships

Financial Resources: managing the business's money and reporting its financial results to management, regulators, and other interested parties

Human Resources: getting, developing, evaluating, compensating, and disciplining the people needed to operate the business

Business Support Resources: providing and managing the facilities, supplies, technology support, management information, and other services needed to run the business effectively

Production and delivery systems: performing services, and/or making or buying products and getting them into the hands of customers

You'll see this "top ten" list again in the next chapter, when we look closely at one of the most important of entrepreneurial skills, that of systemizing the business.

Use the top ten checklist of key external forces to identify opportunities and threats

Opportunities and threats tend to be external forces, most of them beyond your ability to control, but well within your ability to anticipate or react to in ways that can work in your favor. You need to identify them before you can cope with them and turn them to your advantage. You can use the following list to help you recognize the top ten external forces operating on most small businesses.

Laws and regulations: federal, state, and local regulations and regulators can have an enormous impact on the success of your business

The economic situation: the nature of the local economy and how the cycles of economic booms and busts impact your business

Markets: market size, changes in markets, and social changes that can affect your business

Competitors: the entry or exit of competitors in your markets, and the emergence of new kinds of competitors

New products and services: new products can create entire new industries and make others shrink; look at the music industry or telecommunications for dramatic examples in recent years

Technology: not only new products, but also new ways to produce products and services can create enormous opportunities as well as major threats

Public opinion: whether based on fact or perception, public opinion can create major opportunities (hybrid cars, organic foods, diet programs, etc.) or major threats (anti-smoking sentiment, negative perceptions about fast foods, dislike of "big box" stores, etc.)

Resources: availability of skilled workers, communications, transportation, key materials needed by your business, money (availability and cost), utilities (electricity, gas, water, waste disposal, sewage, etc.)

Wild cards: natural events and acts of God (earthquakes, drought, hurricanes, epidemics, etc.) or major accidents

Crime: high crime areas, and vulnerability to white collar crimes

For each of these forces, you need to think about the way it is at the present time, the ways it could change to help or hurt you, and the likelihood that changes could happen.

This all sounds pretty abstract when you're immersed in the day to day management of your business, but they're the kinds of things you need to keep in mind because if you don't, you can miss major opportunities, or be blindsided by events you could have dealt with if you'd seen them coming.

Run some "best case, worst case" scenarios

When identifying strengths and weaknesses, push your thinking by asking yourself, what are the worst things that could happen to the business? Could we deal with them? Why? Why not?

Then ask, "What are the *best* things that could happen to the business? Would we be able to capitalize on those? Why? Why not?

These "best case, worst case" scenarios will push your thinking and help you find vulnerabilities and look at strengths in different ways. Don't get too "out there" with these scenarios. They have to be reasonably possible. If the odds of something happening are a million to one, don't bother to consider it.

Don't narrow your focus too much – stay strategic

Some strengths, weaknesses, opportunities, and threats have a greater impact than others. You'll be tempted to focus on them and ignore some of the lesser ones. You'll probably want to treat the high-impact ones as the "driving" elements in your SWOT analysis. That's usually okay, the most important ones are likely to be the drivers, but that's not always the case. Sometimes the overall pattern tells you more about your situation and the possibilities for your future than a few high-impact SWOTs do. It's one time you have to be careful about the 80/20 rule.

You'll have to use your judgment, but don't be too quick to narrow the scope of your focus. Look for instance at the Johnson's Landscaping example, shown earlier. You could make a case that there are three "driving" SWOTs: (1) the fact that Johnson's is the only landscaping business in the area, (2) that market growth is expected to be dramatic, and (3) that competition is almost certain to move into the market. There's not much doubt that those three are the most high-impact SWOTs on the list. But if you focus primarily on those three factors, you've oversimplified the situation. There's a mixed picture for costs. Plant costs are going down, but labor costs are going up, and the debt service is going to be a drag on profits for five years. What's the net effect on the business, and what can Johnson do about it? If a new competitor moves in and Johnson's primary marketing strength (old lady Johnson herself) is about to retire, how is that going to work out? With growing demand (growing markets), but unreliable suppliers (dirt moving crews and plant availability), how will Johnson's be able to reliably keep up with demand?

Johnson's has a lot of very great strengths, a lot of worrisome weaknesses, and major threats as well as major opportunities. It's not a clear picture, and focusing on only a few factors hides the true nature of the decisions to be made and could (probably would) lead to a troublesome strategy.

Can you see why holistic thinking is such an important part of an entrepreneur's strategic thinking? You have to be aware of the whole picture, not merely some of its more prominent parts.

The beauty of SWOT analysis is that it makes all the forces visible so you can identify them and think about all the possibilities, and ultimately decide on the best strategies for the situation, both long and short term.

The problem is that there's no formula that automatically pops out the right answers; *you* are the formula. Your knowledge of the business and the conditions in which it operates, your knowledge of what you want from the business, and your ability to make the best possible decisions *are* your strategic thinking. That's why this book started out by identifying the habits of mind that block entrepreneurial thinking, and gave you some ways to maximize yours. Your newfound clarity will pay huge dividends in the form of a realistic, achievable strategy, fewer major surprises, and much better ability to deal with the surprises that do occur.

Your SWOT analysis may reveal that some parts of your Strategic Intent may be unfeasible or undesirable. You may uncover opportunities or threats you didn't previously know about, or they may be greater than you thought. It might even happen that the process of thinking through your SWOTs shifted your vision to a more desirable one. While you don't want to change your Strategic Intent for short-term circumstances or shifting thoughts, you should when it's justified. Don't hesitate to make the change when business reasons – major strengths, weaknesses, opportunities, or threats – justify a change.

Strategy is nothing more than a set of decisions you make about your future actions, and of course, strategy is big-picture, not operational details. You'll need to make decisions about creating and developing strengths, eliminating or minimizing weaknesses, taking advantage of opportunities, and avoiding or minimizing the impact of threats. You'll be concerned with anything that helps you develop the various parts of your Strategic Intent such as setting the right goals, establishing the right strategic positioning and differentiation, building the key parts of the business model, and creating the business "personality" you want.

Don't expect one and only one strategy to emerge. As the saying goes, "There's more than one way to skin a cat." There will be any number of possible and even desirable strategies you might pursue (and probably an even greater number of strategies you should avoid). You'll want to create the strategy that gives your business the best chance of reaching the goals you established for your Strategic Intent – the highest profitability, the fastest growth, the greatest market value of the business, the highest ethical standards, the greatest value for customers – whatever you've defined as success for your business. And, of course, your preferences play an important part in your strategy formulation. You're the entrepreneur and you should take your needs and desires into consideration.

There's a universal statement of Strategic Action that applies to every business. It's useful because it sets the framework for you to create your own Strategic Action Statement; the one that applies to your business and its quest to achieve its Strategic Intent.

The Universal Statement of Strategic Action
Our strategy is to develop or maintain key strengths, and eliminate, minimize, or convert key weaknesses (list them and assign target dates for achieving them).
In a nutshell... **Build strengths and eliminate weaknesses**

All you have to do is convert the universal Strategic Action Statement into the *specific* Strategic Action Statement for your business. And how do you do that? You don't have to mention the opportunities or threats because you've already thought about them and made your strategic decisions based on them. You simply list the actions you're going to take in order to build the strengths you'll need and eliminate the weaknesses you won't tolerate, and the timeframe for each.

SWOT Is a State of Mind

SWOT analysis looks like something you do every now and then, maybe yearly, as well as every time something significant happens in your market. You sit down and do a SWOT analysis. And, yes, the first time you do it, that's what you do. Sit down and do a SWOT analysis.

In practice, what happens is very different, at least for the better business leaders. SWOT becomes a mindset, a habit of mind that never stops. The great managers never "do" a SWOT analysis because they're always doing it in their heads, and that's the way it should be. You should keep a steady flow of information coming to you from inside your business and from everywhere outside of your business – from markets, from competitors, from regulators, from community leaders – from everywhere, and you should have a running, continual SWOT *awareness* as an ongoing part of your thinking.

SWOT *analysis* is good, SWOT *awareness* is better. It's the essence of strategic thinking in business, and that's the essence of successful entrepreneurship.

CHAPTER 12

The Inner Workings of a Successful Business

A "Well-Oiled Machine"

As you read this chapter, please keep two key ideas in mind:

Idea #1: Business *principles*, what I think of as the Laws of Nature for Business, are universal. They govern all businesses everywhere, and they are the same for all businesses even though no two businesses are alike.

Idea #2: Business *systems* are the specific ways you put principles to work in *your* business. If you think of a business as an organism – a living creature – you can think of systems as the anatomy of that creature. We create systems, based on universal principles, to do the work of the business and produce the results the business needs to produce, in its specific market, with its specific strategies, in its specific industry, with the specific strengths, weaknesses, and preferences of its management and owners, and within its specific opportunities, constraints, and competitive situation. When we do it right, we've created a creature perfectly adapted for its environment, a successful business.

"Natural Order" and the "Laws of Nature" for Businesses

There is a natural order to any business, large or small, just as there is a natural order for any other kind of "creature." The natural order of a business is governed by business principles; think of them as the "laws of nature for businesses." Most business leaders (the unsuccessful ones) don't follow that natural order, and don't even know there is such a thing. In fact, they develop strategies, make decisions, and take actions that conflict with that natural order, and that's one of the main reasons that small businesses have such a dismal success rate.

What is "natural order"? Think of any living creature, in fact think of the human body, and to make it personal, think of yours. There's a natural order to your body, and it consists of a collection of systems. What is your heart? It's a system for pumping blood. What are your intestines? They're a system for breaking down food for use in all of the body's other systems. What are your muscles? They're systems for applying force to your bones to make them move as you wish them to. What is your eye? It's a system for gathering light and transmitting information back to your brain. You are – and your business is – a system of systems, designed to work together to accomplish your purposes.

If you understand and take advantage of your natural order, you'll live a long, healthy, productive life. If you violate the natural order of your body by abusing your bodily systems – if you eat too much, don't exercise (or over-exercise), subject yourself to too much stress, smoke cigarettes or use other harmful substances, take unnecessary risks, and do any number of harmful or abusive things – then your body will let you down. So, to have a successful body, you need to live a life that follows the basic principles of good mental and physical health. In the same way, it's necessary to follow the basic principles – the natural order – if you're going to have a healthy successful business.

That's fine for managing a business. But what if you're an entrepreneur, responsible for *building* a business – creating it, developing it, nurturing it, and guiding its evolution as it grows? Building a machine is a different proposition from driving a machine that's already built. That's where business *development* principles come into play.

Look at it this way. If you're going to drive an automobile, you don't need to know why it works or how to build it. You only need to know how to operate it so it'll take you where you want to go. But what if you need to **create** an automobile? It's a completely different story. First, you need to know what the automobile will be used for. Do you really need an automobile, or would you be better served by a boat, or a tractor, truck, airplane, or race car? Then you have to design it so it will operate in the conditions you expect and produce the results you need. Designing an effective automobile requires that you understand the laws of physics and chemistry, the properties of materials like steel and rubber, and the processes of using those materials to build something. When it's designed, you have to actually build it by getting all the resources you need, understanding how to shape metal, assembling parts, painting the body, and all the many things that have to be done in order to build a car.

In short, if you're going to create an automobile that does what you want it to do, you have to know the underlying principles of physics and chemistry and how to apply those principles to build the engine, the body, and all the other parts that go into it, and also figure out how to assemble them into a machine that functions as it should.

It's a similar story for an entrepreneur. He has to know what his businesses will do, then he has to design the businesses to do that. When it's designed, he actually has to build it. Then he can "drive" it. Most entrepreneurs think they're driving a business that's like any other business, and all they have to do is figure out the controls and drive. But they're not. They're building a business to do specific work and deliver specific results.

Oh sure, all businesses share similarities, and there's a reason they do. It's because **all businesses are governed by the same "laws of nature."** They all follow the same underlying principles: principles such as revenue minus expenses equals profit; assets minus liabilities equal net worth; customers must be satisfied or they won't buy from you; systemization creates consistency, reduces costs, raises quality, and eliminates confusion and chaos; targeted marketing is more effective than random marketing; and many more.

There's a problem, and it's the universal entrepreneur's problem: you have to apply this natural order to a specific business – *your* business – so that it can be used to ensure success. In our coaching practice, working with many thousands of small businesses, we've figured out how to do it, and our starting point is the "Business Pyramid." The Business Pyramid gives you a way to understand the systems that form the underlying structure – the anatomy – of your business. It reveals the underlying organization of the business and the systems necessary for its health, and it gives you a way to seamlessly put that essential knowledge to work in the real world.

Let's dig a little deeper into the subject of systems before I show you how to use the Business Pyramid to build the systems of your own business.

The Anatomy of a Business: Systems

Bear with me for a moment while I make an academic (but important) point about systems of all kinds, including business systems. At the highest level of systems, we have the universe itself. It's a huge system; the biggest. It has subsystems of galaxies, which in turn have subsystems of planetary systems like our own Solar System, which has subsystems like planets, moons, asteroids, and comets. Our planet Earth has physical systems like the atmosphere, weather, landmasses, oceans, forests, and mountain ranges, and human systems like nations, religions, states, cities, tribes, families, and relationships. Another arrangement of human systems is the system we call the human body, which has subsystems of skeleton, glands, circulation, bones, blood, and the like, and further subsystems of different kinds of cells, and within cells the molecules, then atoms, then subatomic particles that make up atoms, and a succession of even smaller subsystems. The point is this: *the natural order of the universe is systems – actually systems within systems – and businesses are simply one type of system.* From a business perspective, the arrangement of systems consists of the global economy, national economies, industries, businesses, departments within businesses, and down to stores, work teams, jobs, individual workers, and all the many work tasks done by people and machines.

Whenever you look at a specific system in our magnificent hierarchy of systems, you'll find higher level systems and lower level systems above and below the system you're looking at. And that's how it is for a business. No matter what level of system you're looking at, there are always higher systems and lower systems. For instance, here's one chain of business systems: The business itself → the marketing systems within the business → the advertising system within the marketing systems → the ad copy writing system within the advertising systems → the writing supplies system, and if you want to get ridiculous about it →the paper clip organization system. At some point, determined by your judgment and the value of the result, you no longer bother to systemize the work because the result isn't worth the effort it takes to systemize it.

All businesses are alike in that they are subject to the same laws of nature for business, and they have the same natural order. All businesses are also different from each other, in that each business goes about its affairs differently. They have different strategies, different leaders who do things different ways, different products and services, different markets and customers, etc. Both ideas are true – all businesses are alike, and all businesses are different – and there's no paradox or irony if you understand the difference between principles and systems, and how they are interdependent.

> *The underlying principles are the same for <u>all</u> businesses, but the situational factors for <u>each</u> business are different. In order to be successful, a business must create systems that follow the universal business principles <u>and</u> are adapted to the unique circumstances of the individual business.*

Principles → Situational Factors→ Business Systems

Business Pyramid: The Key Business Systems

In my coaching business, we design our coaching practices around the structure of the business itself, so the definition of a business as "...a <u>system</u> for providing <u>value</u> to <u>customers</u>," which you saw earlier when I talked about the top ten business development principles, is the starting point.

A business provides value for customers by doing (and systemizing) four kinds of work:

- Getting customers (marketing work)
- Satisfying customers (production and delivery work)
- Running the business (management work, including leadership)
- Supporting the business (getting and managing the resources needed by the business to do its work, such as people, money, supplies, equipment, etc.).

So the Business Pyramid starts with systems for doing these four kinds of work.

Foundational Systems

The Business Pyramid diagram shows the top level of systems of a business. These are "foundational" systems because they form the foundation of the business. The customer-focused systems – "getting customers" and "satisfying customers" – are the two triangles stacked on each other in the middle of the large pyramid. They are the marketing and production functions of a business. The business-focused systems – "running the business" and "supporting the business" are the two triangles forming the base of the pyramid.

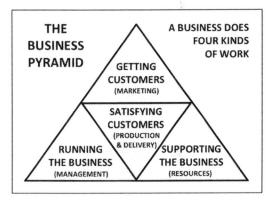

They are the management and resources functions of the business.

The two customer-focused systems deliver value to customers and are the engine that creates profits and the market value of the business itself. Notice that they form a diamond shape in the middle of the pyramid. We call this the "value diamond" because it is here that the business generates value for customers and income for the business. The two business-focused systems support the business overall and enable the value diamond to actually deliver value to customers. We call these two business-focused functions the "pillars of support." The value diamond couldn't stand upright, and the whole pyramid would collapse if the pillars of support were not there to hold them up.

The Ten Strategic Systems

Within the four foundational systems are ten sub-systems that are universal to all businesses. These are "strategic" systems because they form major parts of the business, and the ability of the business to achieve success depends on all of them functioning at high levels of effectiveness. These are the ten categories of strengths and weaknesses you saw earlier as a part of SWOT analysis in the Strategic Action chapter. The ten strategic systems of a business are:

Marketing Systems

- **Market Research:** systematic ways to understand markets, select your target markets, and determine your target customers' needs
- **Marketing Reach:** systematic ways to communicate with your target markets through the right channels with messages that will attract and persuade them
- **Marketing Relationships:** systematic ways to interact directly

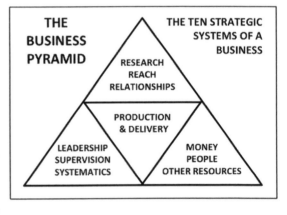

with potential customers, converting them to actual customers, and then managing customer relationships. (You probably think of this as "sales" but the word "sales" has overtones of impersonality and opposition, when in fact you get the best results through a relationship, and a cooperative attitude toward your customers)

Management Systems

- **Leadership**: systematic ways of establishing strategy and business plans, building the business culture, inspiring the business's people to do their best for customers, the business, and themselves, and being a creative force in the business
- **Systematics**: the art and science of systems themselves, working with employees to create systems for doing the work of the business, organizing the business and its systems, viewing the business first as a system of systems, and second as a network of people, and approaching problems as opportunities for creating effective systems rather than occasions for blame and punishment
- **Supervision:** systematic ways of overseeing and mentoring the people in the business, developing them, finding the effective balance of autonomy and micro-management, making the best use of the people of the business, and designing an effective system of rewards and discipline that taps into the motivations of people

Resource Systems

- **Money (Financial Resources):** managing the business's money and reporting its financial results to management and other interested parties
- **People (Humane Resources):** getting, developing, evaluating, compensating, and disciplining the people needed to operate the business
- **Other Resources:** systematic ways of providing and managing the facilities, supplies, technology support, management information, and other services needed to run the business effectively

Production and Delivery Systems: systems for performing services, and/or making or buying products and getting them into the hands of customers

Some of the terms I've used may be unfamiliar to you, but I use them for a purpose. For instance, "marketing reach" includes all the ways the business reaches out to customers and potential customers, such as advertising, public relations, web sites, and the like. Marketing reach is one-way communication designed to attract customers to you and your products. "Marketing relationships" are all those activities that happen when a connection has been made with a potential customer: sales, customer information, demonstrations, and any other activity that is interactive with customers and potential customers. "Humane resources" is more than a play on the word humane. It is a reminder of the double vision that, while one view of the people of the business is that of productive assets to be deployed where they'll be most effective, people must first and foremost be valued as individuals deserving of respect and compassion. "Systematics" is an expansion of the word "systematic" and means the management practice of developing, installing, and monitoring business systems.

Every successful business – no matter what size, industry, or location – has these systems, and numerous supporting sub-systems within them. They're essential for the natural order of the business to operate. There may not be separate people assigned to these functions, in fact, in a one-person business, that one person does everything. Whether there are one or one thousand or one hundred thousand people in a business, the same strategic systems are needed – maybe simple and small in one business, and large and complicated in another business – but the systems must be there and must operate effectively, or the business can't succeed.

There's a lot of science to systems, and people get college degrees and advanced degrees on the subject, but you don't have to do that to make effective use of systems. All you need is a few basic ideas to get you started. So let me wrap up this chapter with a starter course in system design.

How to build a system: the basics

Up to this point I've been telling you about systems from a strategic thinking point of view. But the systems that actually do the work of the business are operational, not strategic. Strategic thinking about systems is essential, and it's what most small business leaders don't know how to think about, but it's the detailed, operational thinking that puts systems into place and gets the work of the business done.

Systems (as well as sub-systems, and each of the work steps within a system) have three components: inputs (the resources needed to produce the result), processes (the work that must be done to produce the result), and outputs (the results generated by the system; what it must produce).

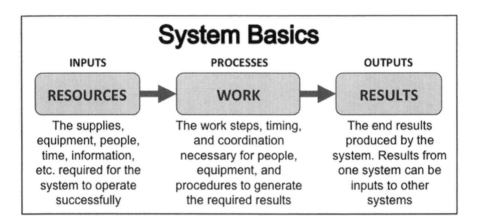

The general approach to creating a system starts at the end. Basically, the thinking is this:

1. First, define (precisely) the **results** the system must produce.
2. Secondly, determine what **work steps** are needed to get those results.
3. Finally, determine what **resources** are necessary to do the work.

A system is identified by the result it produces, but there is an unlimited number of systems that could be created to produce any one result. For example, every business needs selling systems, but each business creates its own selling systems based on it's own requirements and resources, and based on the characteristics of its products and customers. The selling systems created by your neighborhood plumbing service will be vastly different from those created by the worldwide Coca Cola Company, and that's as it should be because they have different markets, competitors, regulations, products, strategies, and owners. Yet both businesses will have essential systems for communicating with potential customers, for attracting them, and for creating the products and services that will satisfy them. It's a law of nature for business – a business principle – that all businesses need selling systems, but it is also true that the specific selling systems created by each business will be designed for the situation faced by that business. The various systems may bear little resemblance to each other, yet they'll serve the same strategic purpose for the business and its customers.

System design starts with a picture: a system map

Your first visualization of a system should be a simple diagram – a map of sorts – that shows the work steps and how they relate to each other. You should sketch your systems maps by hand and in pencil so you can adjust them as you think about the steps. It can be as simple as this map for washing your dishes at home after dinner (assuming you have a dishwasher).

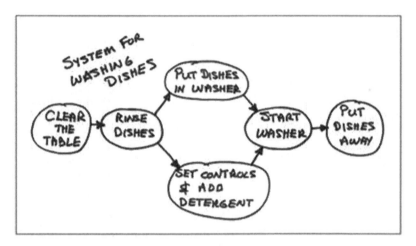

Don't number the work steps until you have completed your system map. If you number them, it'll limit your thinking because you'll tend to think they have to go in numerical order, and that may not be the case. Look at the dishwashing example. Can you think of several different ways to do the job? For instance, you can set the washer's controls and put in the detergent at any time, can't you? And, do you really have to rinse the dishes before washing them? If you have two people doing the job, couldn't you be doing two tasks at once, and therefore getting the work done faster?

You can see that, even in the simple dishwashing example, mapping the work makes you think about all kinds of possibilities; that's the whole point. In your business, you want to get the job done in the best, most cost-effective way. In other words, look at all possible ways to do it and choose the system that does the best job. If you simply make a list of the work to be done, you constrain your thinking to the list, which tends to limit your thinking and short-circuit your intuition.

The tech-savvy among you may want to do your mapping on the computer, but it's usually more efficient to use paper and pencil first, and save the computer diagrams for the documentation. Why? Because pencil and paper are quicker and more flexible, and they don't force you to conform to the structured process imposed by the limitations of the computer. With simple paper and pencil tools, your thinking tends to be focused directly on the system, and not so much on the computer manipulations necessary to construct the boxes and arrows and text placement of the diagram. You can very quickly grab a blank sheet of paper, draw boxes (or circles) and arrows, erase them and draw new ones, or scribble over them. In other words, use whatever method that allows you to think quickly and both intuitively and analytically. If you can do that on a computer without giving in to the linear/analytical nature of the machine, that's fine. Most of us are more effective using our whole-minds directly, rather than filtered through the structure imposed on us through the computer.

My purpose here is not to train you in the intricacies of systems design, but to jump-start your thinking so that you can do a reasonable job of identifying and developing the systems you'll need in order to launch, or re-launch, your business. The most important step for a would-be entrepreneur is to be aware of the need for and benefits of systemization in the business, and a basic understanding of what systemization is all about. Once you're aware, your newly developing entrepreneurial habits of mind will include systemization, and it'll become part of both your strategic and operational thinking, which is yet another form of double vision.

CHAPTER 13
Concluding Thoughts

In this book, you probably found more psychology, brain/mind science, and self-analysis than you expected. It's not like most business-focused books, is it? The business people and entrepreneurs that I've known have tended to be no-nonsense, get-it-done people, not prone to navel-gazing. They're all about action, not analysis, and results, not reflection. If you're like that, and you probably are, then your first reaction when you noticed this book and glanced at the table of contents was probably skepticism and doubt.

But, for some reason, something about this book suggested that my approach of mind first, then business might hold some of the keys to the kingdom for you. It might even have been an *unconscious* reaction on your part, heaven forbid.

Somehow, for the short time it took you to decide to buy this book, you became intrigued by its premise: **You must master your mind if you want to master your business.**

As a matter of fact, I originally began to write a book about thinking and the mind. But it was too abstract, too academic. Thinking about the mind doesn't work for most people, especially action oriented people. There needs to be an injection of reality, of something specific, something to focus the mind not on the mind but on how to put it to use on something real, something practical. You can study a box of tools but until you actually put the tools to use, you don't understand them. You can read about baking a cake, but until you actually bake one you don't really "get it." So my book on thinking and the mind had to focus on something useful and real and had to get you to immerse yourself in it, not just study it.

Why entrepreneurship?

My background is in business, and for the past two decades my focus has been small businesses and entrepreneurship, so that became the focus of attention in this book. Small businesses were my living laboratory and my university, and they allowed me legitimately to claim credibility in the field of entrepreneurship. But really, the bulk of this book is actually about living in reality, and taking control of that amazing mind of yours. If the context had been dentistry, farming, clothing design, or any other life endeavor, then the book would have been a manual for becoming a consummate dentist, farmer, designer, or whatever, and the premise would have been, *You must master your mind if you want to master [fill in the blank].*

So don't be fooled. This is a book about getting control of your *life* by getting control of your thinking; business is merely one way to apply that thinking. That's why, in our coaching business we found that as our clients' businesses got better, so did the other aspects of their lives. When you think about it, it should come as no surprise that better *lives* are the primary result of improved habits of mind, and better entrepreneurship is merely a side effect. The mind/business connection is actually a mind/life connection, and entrepreneurship is simply one aspect of life, albeit an important one.

I've made a prediction to myself about the people who buy this book. I've predicted that more than half of you won't really engage in the work that I've outlined. Either you won't really believe it, or you'll be too impatient, or you'll cherry pick a few ideas that seem useful, or you'll think you "get it" when in fact you don't. You'll let your habits of mind continue to get in your way. You'll continue to believe that you long ago mastered the art/science/skill of perceiving reality as it is. You won't buy into the idea that your mind distorts things routinely and you'll continue to believe beyond any doubt, right down to the tips of our toes, that the Reality B that lives in your mind *is* Reality A. Part of that reality is that your conscious mind is now and always has been in charge of your life. Your me-bias and self-perception will tell you that you already knew all that stuff about the dozen distortions and, while others are guilty, you certainly haven't fallen into any of those traps.

I've also predicted to myself that a minority of you *will* engage in the work in this book (at least some of it) and come to the realization that you really haven't been in charge of your own thinking for all these years, at least not consciously. You've routinely distorted reality, clung to personality habits that have sometimes blocked or retarded your success, and you've been blind to it all, blaming circumstances when things didn't turn out as you wanted them to, and hoping for a breakthrough or a streak of luck to turn things around.

I have high expectations for this (hopefully large) minority, and they (hopefully you) are why I wrote the book in the first place. It's deeply embedded in my Core Purpose that I want this book to make a difference in as many lives as possible. I want to help as many people as I can to become true entrepreneurs, and in doing so, help them make the kinds of contributions to the world that can be made only by an entrepreneur's mind. When you think about it, entrepreneurial thinking has built the world we live in, and will build the world of the future.

I've been purposefully repetitious about one point in this book, and that point is this: When you take on these new habits of mind, at first they feel wrong, awkward, sometimes embarrassing, and oh-so-slow and unnatural. You have to engage them, practice them, in your mind and for real, over and over again until they become innate, automatic, and unconscious. You have to consciously and conscientiously discipline yourself to make them into the new habits of mind that they need to be. I've led you to expect that, with enough practice, each will become a new habit of mind, and that's true, but there's a greater benefit.

Collectively, and over time (not too much time), all of these new habits of mind will interrelate and integrate in both your conscious and unconscious mind, until, ultimately, clarity will be your new normal. That may not sound like much, but given your starting point (and mine), it's actually miraculous. There are so very many ways that your mind can and does distort your thinking and cause you to cling to your dysfunctional personality habits that, when your new norm becomes clarity, everything opens up for you. In fact an appropriate title for this book (if I hadn't chosen to focus on entrepreneurship) would have been *Clarity: Getting Reality Right.*

I want to reinforce one more point before you close this book. As I said earlier I don't believe in transformation except for caterpillars and tadpoles. I'm not asking you to transform into something you're not. I'm talking about authenticity. If you engage in the work I've described in these pages, you won't be transformed into somebody new. That's impossible anyway. You'll uncover the authentic you, the real you who has been buried under decades of conditioning and the sometimes tyranny of your own mind.

All I've really done with this book is give you a manual for taking control of your mind and returning to the authentic you, plus some essential ideas about business strategy to keep it focused on entrepreneurship.

I wanted to end this book with something profound, but you know what? That's for you to do. It's all up to you and always has been. Finding your deepest source of motivation, clarifying your thinking, finding ways to see reality as it actually is, seeing yourself as you really are, thinking strategically when you need to, and shifting your personality so that it's more in tune with who you really are and works better in the real world; those are all up to you.

I wish you well.

ATTACHMENT A

How I Learned All This Stuff, and Why I Know It Works

I'll start with a little bit of history and then describe how entrepreneurial thinking and the mind/business connection can be developed in anyone who's willing by telling you how it's working for thousands and thousands of small business owners and managers.

For me, it all began twenty years ago, in 1995, when I joined Michael Gerber and his team of small business coaches, then calling themselves the Gerber Business Development Company. Everybody should have a Michael Gerber in his life. Michael is irascible, demanding, impatient, and simply cannot pass up an opportunity; he's the consummate entrepreneur. He's also brilliant, deeply compassionate and loving, not to mention impish and more than a little profane. To this day I both love and hate him, and he knows it. I suspect he wouldn't have it any other way.

If you want to get a sense of Michael's thinking, and the principles that underlie good business development, you've got to read his book, *The E-Myth Revisited.* It's a must-read for business people and would-be entrepreneurs, and, according to the Wall Street Journal, it's the all-time best-selling book on small business management.

Business coaching is the practice of teaching others how to create and manage businesses, and mentoring them through the process to success. That's what we were doing in those days, but at a deeper level we were doing something else as well, something more important and fundamental. We were helping our clients shift their conscious and unconscious habits of mind. While we were teaching business principles and helping our clients apply them to their businesses, we were also helping them overcome their unconscious thinking, shifting their beliefs, replacing dysfunctional habits of mind with new ones, and tapping into their most deeply held sense of purpose and motivation. In other words, using business as the focus of attention, we enabled them to convert their flawed thinking and entrepreneurial illusions into the beginnings of true entrepreneurship. And it was no small thing that, as we helped our clients improve their businesses, they reported to us that their lives outside of their businesses also improved.

Michael Gerber was the pioneer in this kind of business coaching, beginning in the 1970s and continuing to this day. I joined him in the mid-1990s, and was the catalyst for creating his leading-edge, never-been-done-before E-Myth Mastery Program. It was my job to create the written materials and practices that hundreds of small business coaches used daily to teach and mentor thousands and thousands of clients, in all industries, and in a dozen nations around the world. I converted the practical knowledge hard won by Michael and his team over the decades into a disciplined program, teachable by any coach and useable by any client.

And it worked. Beautifully. At the time, it was the most advanced coaching method available anywhere. Michael's organization, rebranded as the E-Myth Academy, became the preeminent small business coaching organization in the world.

I left Michael Gerber's organization in the year 2000, after completing the E-Myth Mastery program for him. My work there was complete, so I moved into academia, where I taught business management and leadership at Menlo College and Santa Clara University, both in California's Silicon Valley. Business principles are business principles no matter where you learn them, so much of my teaching was pretty straightforward, similar to teaching engineering. But leadership teaching was something very different, very personal. My favorite was a course called "Leadership, Creativity, and Ethics" which relied on many of the principles and practices you'll find in this book (entrepreneurs are a very special kind of leader). I taught college kids and, in the adult education program, working adults of all ages and in a wide variety of occupations, all of them wanting to create the best possible lives for themselves.

The results were bimodal; either spectacularly successful, or a complete bust. The people who engaged in the process – the ones who were willing to learn new habits of mind and open themselves up to new possibilities – did well. The students who regarded the work as tasks to be completed for a grade or to please a teacher made little or no progress. In business coaching, the unengaged people were the people who dropped out of the coaching program after a few months, making no progress, and believing the program had failed them. In reality they had failed themselves by giving in to their old habits of mind, always looking for the easy shortcut, and in doing so, perpetuating business-as-usual, and more disappointingly, life-as-usual.

Those who engaged in the process put themselves on the path to leadership and entrepreneurship, and made strides in their personal lives as they did so. The successful students gave me feedback testifying to better grades and a more successful classroom experience. The adult education students reported more success in their jobs, as well as feedback from coworkers and bosses that showed that their business skills and their leadership potential had improved, often remarkably so. And, in the earlier years with Michael Gerber, the small business owners we coached found themselves becoming better business leaders, with successful, growing businesses.

Two examples:

"John" was a worker in a local municipal government. After about three weeks in my Leadership, Creativity, and Ethics course, John told me that his coworkers were telling him they had noticed improvements in his attitude, helpfulness, and general approach to his work. After about five weeks, he reported that his boss was saying the same thing. By the end of the 12-week course, John reported that he had been promoted to a managerial position. John credited the course for his improvements.

"Jane," a personal organization consultant, reported conflicts between her and her most important client, and that she was expecting the client to fire her soon. At about the fifth week of the course, Jane reported that her client had noticed a sharp improvement in Jane's services and attitude, and not only increased her usage of Jane's services but also referred Jane to her friends.

In 2005, I left academia and formed a team of experienced business coaches in the USA and Australia, raised the necessary startup money, and launched a new company, doing business as the Full Spectrum Coaching Company. Our objective was, and still is, to help small business owners worldwide improve their businesses, and in doing so, improve their lives. My first task was to create an entirely new, leading-edge coaching program. It took four years of development, experimentation, and writing, but we pulled it off. The result is the Full Spectrum Business Development Program, and by all reports from users it's superior to anything else in the field of business coaching.

So, that's the history.

But the question is, does this stuff work? And how does it work? How does it help you escape your counterproductive habits of mind and convert them into entrepreneurial thinking? How does it help you escape the illusion of entrepreneurship, and become a true entrepreneur rather than a wannabe? How does it create a mind/business connection and give you the entrepreneur's edge?

Here's how the process is working in a coaching environment, in the real world, for our business clients. (In this book, I've streamlined and condensed much of the process, so you can do it for yourself.)

First of all, and not surprisingly, our successful clients are the ones who engage in the process. They don't have to be fully convinced the program will work, as long as they're open to that possibility, and willing, honestly, to "give it a shot." Those who simply sign up to get someone else to fix their businesses aren't really engaged in the process. They just go through the motions, and come out of the process the same as they went in, a little bit older, but none the wiser.

"Engage in the process" means that they have to try some new ways of thinking and act on those new thoughts. In order to do that they have to become more open to possibilities than they've been in the past, they have to look more critically at the realities of their businesses and themselves, and they have to think outside of the box, entrepreneurially.

To do the work of fixing their businesses, our clients first take a quick look inside themselves (first your mind then your business). We help them discover their deeply held inner motivation, their "Core Purpose," which I tell you about in this book. They sometimes do this skeptically, not initially seeing the value in it, but giving it a try anyway. Those who are engaged in the process come away with something precious; a bedrock source of purpose and motivation in their lives. The unengaged ones go through the motions, but in actuality, they never really "get it."

Next, we ask our clients to take their minds out of their daily grind and think about general business principles. I think of them as the "laws of nature for business." It's the beginning of strategic thinking, and it's a fundamental aspect of the entrepreneurial mind. We start them off by suggesting some new beliefs and ways of thinking that open them up to more possibilities than they were accustomed to imagining.

Then we get specific and focus on the client's own business, seeing how the laws of nature for business apply in their unique situations. We do this through a series of practices with names like "Strategic Intent" (thinking about what they want the business to look like when it's mature and successful), "Strategic Action" (making the right strategic decisions about the business), and more. What's happening is that by doing the work of developing their businesses, they're developing new, entrepreneurial, habits of thinking. They don't set out to create new ways of thinking, but that's what they're unconsciously doing as they work on their businesses through practice, repetition, and the willingness to try new ideas.

The longer they stay in the program, experimenting with new beliefs about business and about themselves, practicing new habits of mind by doing the work of building their businesses, and shedding huge chunks of their unproductive thinking in favor of a new, entrepreneurial mindset, the more they develop.

Yes, of course their businesses get better – much better – but more importantly, so do their *lives*.

The practices I'm offering you work, but only if you engage them. If you merely go through the motions, you'll waste your time and make little or no progress toward entrepreneurial thinking and business success, and you'll blame me for offering something that you think doesn't work. If you don't engage, your old habits of mind will continue to dominate, and you'll get the same results that you've always gotten in your career and your life. That's okay with me if it's okay with you, but it's regrettable because so much more is possible.

ATTACHMENT B

The 8-Sense Experience – _Re_-Living and _Pre_-Living the Events of Your Life

We have five senses: sight, hearing, touch, smell, and taste. Each sense is a pathway for information to get into our minds. The five senses provide the raw material for our perceptions of what's real, our Reality B (remember that Reality A is the actual reality that exists in the real world outside of our minds, and Reality B is our internal perception of that reality; they often are not the same).

Thoughts, emotions, and bodily sensations aren't really senses, they're mental activities that enable us to "make sense" of our experiences by reacting to and interpreting the information brought to us by our five actual senses. Thoughts and emotions are familiar to all of us, but you may not have paid much attention to your bodily sensations, so let me say more about them.

The bodily sensations I'm talking about originate in our minds but we feel them in our bodies. The tingling that accompanies fear or anger; the light, open feeling parents get while looking at their sleeping children; the heavy, leaden feeling many of us get when we're dreading something; the electric sensation we get when we're startled; that sinking feeling in the pit of the stomach that signals tension and anxiety; and any number of other bodily sensations we get in response to conscious and unconscious thoughts and impressions. There are other ways the mind translates conscious and unconscious thinking into the body, for instance the movement of muscles in response to the mind's intentions.

I have the thought, "I'll pick up that spoon," and my mind unconsciously directs the right muscles to move in such a way that I pick up the spoon. Another mind-body connection is the so-called placebo effect, in which the beliefs of the mind influence the operation of the immune system and some healing processes. There are others, and science is beginning to understand the mechanisms by which some of these mind-body phenomena work. So the fact that we have bodily sensations that originate in the mind should come as no surprise to you.

You live your life in these eight "dimensions" of experience which are sight, hearing, touch, taste, and smell, plus the three interpretive functions expressed as thoughts, emotions, and bodily sensations, all of which, collectively, I call the "8-sense experience."

Your entire life has been, and will continue to be, an extended 8-sense experience.

So what? Why is the 8-sense experience a valuable tool in your efforts to develop useful habits of mind and to create within you the most accurate possible Reality B? The short answer is that the 8-sense experience allows you to become aware of your unconscious habits of mind and the triggers that set them in motion, and that awareness enables your conscious mind to take charge of those habits and change the ones that aren't working for you. In other words, the 8-sense experience helps you access your unconscious thinking and gives you a way to reshape your unconscious habits of mind.

To explain, let me first remind you that your habits of mind are mostly unconscious, were mostly unconsciously developed, and are anchored to your unconscious ways of thinking, believing, and feeling. Some of them, mainly your personality habits, are deeply anchored in your earliest childhood experiences. The 8-sense experience is a way to mentally re-live events in your past, and unlike mere remembering, put you in touch with the conscious and unconscious associations that occurred in the original experience. No, the re-experienced event in your mind won't be as intense or fully experienced as the original one was, but if you immerse yourself in it, and bring forth as much of the 8-sense impact as you can, it'll bring back many of the stronger impressions, and allow you to get access to much of the unconscious part of the original experience; not all of it, but a lot, and enough to give you access to and make you consciously aware of much of the unconscious workings of your habits of mind.

That's the value of the 8-sense _re_-experience; it enables you to relive the disappointing events of your life in such a way that you become consciously aware of your counterproductive habits of mind, and that awareness gives you the leverage to shift them into something more productive. Furthermore, an 8-sense visualization of a future experience – an 8-sense _pre_-experience – gives you a way to mentally practice new habits of mind and integrate them into your ways of thinking and being. You can actually use your imagination to practice new behaviors, in the privacy of your own mind, with none of the risk of failure or embarrassment that so often arise from changing a habit when you're new at it and probably clumsy and hesitant. This imaginary practice, believe it or not, changes your brain by beginning to create new connections – new brain circuitry – that, with repetition and practice, will in a short time become new and improved habits of mind. In other words, you'll learn to think better and more clearly, both consciously and unconsciously.

Let me summarize: An 8-sense _re_-experience can enable you to mentally relive a past experience and bring much of the unconscious parts of that experience into your conscious awareness so that you can identify and understand your unproductive habits of mind. Furthermore, you can redesign your own habits of mind and use the 8-sense _pre_-experience to practice new ways of thinking and being until they replace old, unproductive habits. You can actually re-program yourself, and the 8-sense pre-experience helps you do it.

Another thing to consider is "triggers." Habits are bundles of neural activity, which get triggered (consciously or unconsciously), and then automatically go into action, and run their course. An 8-sense re-experience allows you to discover your triggers at the same time you're discovering the habits they set in motion.

Why are triggers important? When you know what triggers a habit of mind, you can use that trigger as an alert, which tells you when to consciously interrupt an unproductive habit, and, still consciously, redirect your thinking and behavior into more productive thoughts and actions. In short order, you break the old habit, and a new, improved habit becomes anchored to the old trigger. You'll see what I mean below as you look more closely at the 8-sense experience.

All of that was a long way to say that the 8-sense experience – whether <u>re</u>-experience or <u>pre</u>-experience – enables you to understand your unproductive habits of mind and to identify what triggers them into action. Let me show you how it works with an example. In this case I'll use the example of "John," who wants to re-experience a disappointing event in his life so he can discover the unproductive habits of mind that produced the disappointment. By the way, you can have an 8-sense re-experience by yourself, but it's usually better to be "coached" by a trusted friend or advisor, and the example below includes John's friend Jane, who coaches him through the experience.

The process is pretty simple, although, as I've said repeatedly, at first it'll be awkward and slow, like any new skill you take on. First you choose a place and time when you won't be interrupted or distracted for about 15 to 30 minutes, then you recall a time in your life when you were unsuccessful or when things fell significantly short of your expectations, and then you mentally immerse yourself in the experience, re-living in your mind as much of the sights, sounds, smells, tastes, textures, thoughts, emotions, and bodily sensations as you are able to bring forth.

Here goes. It's a rather long tale and it'll help if you try to "get into" the thinking of John and Jane without injecting your own thoughts and experiences.

Jane: *Okay John, close your eyes and relax (Jane pauses while John settles in).*

John: *I'm ready.*

Jane: *You said that the experience you want to explore is the time when you went to your boss to ask for a pay raise but were severely criticized by him and denied the raise. Is that right?*

John: *Right.*

Jane: *To get the process started, and to set the scene, think back to the moments just before you met with your boss, and quickly remember the experience from start to finish. Let me know when you're done. (Jane waits... it takes less than a minute)*

John: *Got it.*

Jane: *For the next few minutes, I'm going to prompt you to re-live the details of that scene so that you'll be mentally immersed in it, and as close to your original state of mind as you can get. This is the 8-sense re-experience we talked about.*

    For about 5 minutes, Jane prompted John to recall and re-experience everything about the meeting with his boss by asking questions such as: What was the scene? What do you remember seeing? What was around you? What did your boss look like? What was he wearing? What was on his desk? Was the lighting bright or dim? What objects did you notice around the room? (Jane pauses to allow John to fully re-experience the visual impressions of the event.) What did your boss's voice sound like? Were there any other sounds like air conditioning, auto traffic outside, sounds from outside his office, rustling of your or his clothing, tapping of pencils or fingers, or any other sounds? (pause...) Were there any odors, pleasant or unpleasant? (pause...) Recall the feeling of your feet on the floor and your butt in the chair. Were you warm or cool? Do you remember how the chair felt, or the slight pressure of your shirt collar on your neck, or the pressure of your boss's hand as you shook hands? Were there any other sensations of touch or texture? (pause...) Were there any tastes associated with the meeting, such as coffee or other refreshment? (pause...) What thoughts were going through your head as you approached your boss's door, and as the meeting started? Were you worried? Were you confident or uneasy? Did you have any scenarios running through your mind? Did your thinking change as the meeting progressed? (pause...) What was your emotional state? Were you anxious, happy or sad, nervous, or feeling any other emotion? Look carefully for hints of emotion that you might not have noticed at the time, or that you were suppressing. Did your emotions change as you entered your boss's office, and as the meeting moved along? (pause...) Did you have any bodily sensations, such as tightness anywhere, tingling, the urge to yawn, bodily heaviness or lightness, stomach uneasiness, anything around your solar plexus...anything at all however slight, however unimportant? (pause...)

Jane: *Are you fully immersed in the experience?*

John: *Yes. Let's continue.*

Jane: *Okay. In the days or hours before the meeting with your boss, what were your expectations for the meeting? Not your hopes but your expectations. And how confident were you about your expectations?* [Note: This seems to interrupt the process by injecting conscious thoughts from an earlier point in time, but not only does it reactivate John's expectations, it also allows his unconscious mind to continue to re-engage with the experience of the meeting. It also helps him recall his Reality B at the time, which was certainly distorted, otherwise the meeting would have produced the expected results.]

John: *I was pretty sure I'd get a pay raise, and maybe even a promotion. For the past couple of months, I'd been performing well above the level of my coworkers, my boss seemed more positive about me, my work brought in a lot of new customers, my coworkers seemed nicer to me than usual, and I felt pretty good about everything at work. I didn't realize it at the time, but re-experiencing it made me remember that I had been feeling more energetic in those days, and in a generally good mood most of the time. I remember occasionally feeling a bit "off" when I first went in to the office some mornings, and sometimes I felt a bit "down," but that happens to me now and then and it wasn't anything to pay attention to. So, yeah, I was pretty confident, maybe a little bit nervous, but that happens to anybody asking his boss for a raise, doesn't it? My specific expectation was that my boss would agree to give me a raise, maybe even on the spot during the meeting, and that I'd get some strongly positive feedback.*

Jane: *So, what happened?*

John: *My boss asked me to sit in the chair in front of his desk, and then he said, "You asked for this meeting so it's your agenda, John. When you're done, I have some things I've been meaning to say to you, but let's start with your concerns. So...what's up?" I remember now, but didn't notice it at the time, that he smiled at me, but it was kind of a tight smile, and the energy in the room was slightly uncomfortable, maybe even a bit tense.*

I started off by mentioning my excellent performance over the past months, the fact that I had brought in a lot of new customers, the way my coworkers seemed more respectful of me these days, and how I felt like everything was going well for me.

As I talked, my boss's expression got tighter, and he went all stony-faced. It surprised me because I would have thought he'd be all smiles, and would have given me a compliment or two. When I asked about the possibility of a raise in pay, he actually frowned.

That worried me, and the awkward silence that followed worried me even more. I remember thinking to myself, "What's going on? This isn't at all what I expected."

Then he shocked me. He said, "John, that's not going to happen. I'll be blunt. The fact is that you're in danger of losing your job if your attitude and your performance don't improve. That's what I planned on talking with you about."

Then he stunned me even more. He said that my performance was well below satisfactory, that the number of customers I had brought in was high but they were the wrong kinds of customers (low profit margins from their business, they were demanding and hard to deal with, and they didn't stay with us very long), and that my coworkers had been going out of their way to be nice to me because they all saw how I was floundering and they didn't want to make me feel bad. They were actually embarrassed and felt sorry for me. He wrapped up by saying, "John, I'm bewildered that you could be so blind to your own shortcomings and poor performance, and so badly misread the signs of your incompetence."

Then he said that he needed to think about the situation for a while, and that he'd schedule another meeting soon to talk with me about a remedial program to get my performance up to snuff, and what would happen if I didn't improve. He closed the meeting asking me to take a day off to think about how I could so badly have misunderstood the situation, and to come up with some ideas to improve my performance.

Jane: *How awful for you.*

John: *Yeah, it was really bad.*

Jane: *What happened afterwards?*

John: *We met two days later. I had thought long and hard about the situation, and was trying to get him to understand why he was mistaken, but he wasn't open to what I had to say. In fact he got really angry. You know how some people just can't see reality, and can't accept responsibility for their actions? That was him. It was a very short meeting, and he fired me, on the spot, before I could finish what I wanted to say.*

    I cleaned out my desk under the supervision of a security officer, left the building, and that was the last I saw of him or anyone else in the company. It was a gross injustice, and I have to admit that, even now, three years later, I'm still bitter about it.

Jane: *John, you've done a good job re-living that disappointment. Our purpose is to look back at the experience to discover if any of your habits of mind contributed to the unexpectedly bad outcome. So now, while it's all still vivid in your mind, let's dig into your thinking and see what we can discover.*

John: Okay.

Jane: First of all, before we start, you'd have to agree that your under-standing – your Reality B – didn't match up with the situation, did it? If it had, everything would have turned out as you expected, right?

John: Yeah, my boss had a completely weird perception of my performance, and I had no clue that he felt that way. His Reality B was that he was disappointed in me, even though I didn't deserve it, and my Reality B was that he and my coworkers were pleased with my work. And as we know, Reality A, the truth of the matter, was that my performance was pretty good.

Jane: Okay, let's start with your boss's Reality B. In order to get the most out of re-living the experience, I'm going to ask you to become an impartial referee, and look at the experience from the point of view of somebody who was a complete stranger, who knew neither you nor your boss, and who knew nothing of the situation. You'll have to be completely neutral, and that's not an easy task, especially when you feel that you've been wronged. I want you to become completely objective about your boss, as if you were a third person watching the meeting with no prior opinions about either you or him. It means that you have to let go of your natural me-bias for a while. Can you do that?

John: Of course I can.

Jane: Don't be so quick to agree. Knowing about your me-bias and avoid-ing its distortions aren't so easy. You have to become a critic, almost as if you're fault-finding about yourself. At this point you're sure you were right, but to truly understand the situation and your boss's attitude, you also have to be willing to see the opposite point of view and be a fault-finder about yourself. You don't have to believe it, but you need to see it. Can you really do that?

John: When you put it like that, maybe it's not so easy, but I'll give it a try. I'd appreciate it if you'd help keep me on track if you see my me-bias taking charge.

Jane: Of course I will. Now remember, you're taking the point of view of a third person, observing the meeting with no previous opinions.

John: Okay.

Jane: I noticed a number of things you said that we could take a look at. Let's start with the fact that you had developed more new customers than the other employees. How did you know that was true?

John: We get weekly reports showing sales results for all of us. I consistently, probably more than half the time, got higher numbers of new customers than anyone else.

Jane: Was there anything else on that report?

John: Sure. It showed customer retention, customer complaints, the profitability of each customer relationship, and a demographic profile of the customers brought in by each salesperson. But the number we all looked at was the number of new customers. It's been that way at every company I've ever worked for.

Jane: Is there another way to look at that report?

John: Sure, but new customers are the key to success.

Jane: Didn't your boss say that the customers you brought in were, let me look at my notes, the wrong kinds of customers because they generated low profit margins from their business, were demanding, hard to deal with, and they didn't stay with you very long?

John: Well…yeah, but everybody knows what's really important. Bring in lots of customers and everything is great.

Jane: Would an unbiased third party observer agree with you?

John: Sure.

Jane: Really...?

John: Well...I think so...

Jane: Keep that in mind, and let's move on to the next point. You said that your coworkers seemed nicer to you than usual, and you felt pretty good about everything at work, but your boss said that your coworkers had been going out of their way to be nice because they all saw how you were floundering and they didn't want to make things worse for you. They were actually embarrassed and felt sorry for you.

John: Yeah. My boss seemed to genuinely believe what he was saying, but I knew better. He was simply wrong.

Jane: What would an objective observer think?

John   He wouldn't know what to think. He'd see both of us, and know that each one of us believed his perceptions were true. It's conflicting Reality B's isn't it? I know my view was right, but an observer wouldn't know that. He'd probably be confused and want more information.

Jane: What kind of information?

John: Well, something that showed that one point of view – one Reality B – was closer to the truth than the other.

Jane: What about your own experience, for instance the signals you were getting that you didn't pay attention to. You said that you get them from time to time, but don't pay much attention to them because they're not important. Remember, you said that sometimes you felt *"off" or "down" when you got into the office in the morning, and you also felt nervous going into the meeting with your boss. You didn't feel that they were anything you needed to pay attention to, so you didn't look into them to figure out what caused them. Could those have been emotional signals that things were not as they seemed?*

John: *No. I get them all the time, and they don't amount to anything.*

Jane: *Remember when we talked about triggers and alerts? How the unconscious mind communicates with the conscious mind with thoughts, emotions, and bodily sensations when it is conflicted or when things don't add up? Is there a possibility of that happening to you in this experience? You don't have to believe it's true, but try to be open to the possibility.*

John: *Jane, this is pretty far-fetched, isn't it? I know what I know.*

Jane: *You may be right but let's test it. Remember to stay in your objective point-of-view, observing your inner workings as if you were a third person who could read your mind. Go back to one of the times you went to the office and it felt "off." Re-live the "off" feeling fully, in the 8-sense way, and think about the feeling and what might have caused it. Talk me through your thoughts.*

John: *Okay. I'll re-live a Monday morning a week or two before the meeting with my boss. The "off" feeling happened mostly on Mondays, I guess because it was a fresh immersion into the office atmosphere after a weekend of relaxation. I walked in the office, saying hello to everyone as I passed them on the way to my desk. They all looked up and smiled, saying something pleasant as I passed, so I dropped the "off" feeling and got on with my day.*

Jane: *Good. Now go back in your mind again and try to experience the facial expressions, tone of voice, choice of words of each of your coworkers, one at a time, in slow motion.*

John: Okay, I'm doing that.

Jane: [pause...] What are you noticing?

John: Nothing much.

Jane: What?

John: Well, I don't know what it is, but each of them was pleasant and friendly enough, but something about them wasn't quite right. It wasn't anything obvious, but, I don't know, something made me feel momentarily down, almost sad. It was quick, and passed immediately, in fact at the time I didn't even notice it, but it was there.

     Am I making this up because you're asking me all these questions?

Jane: No, you're not making anything up. It was your unconscious mind sending you subtle signals because something might really have been off, and it was not consistent with your expectations or your mental model of what should have been happening. Instead of pausing to figure out what the underlying cause was and if it was anything to be concerned about, you did what you always do, which was not to notice the signals and get on with your day.

     So, while you're still immersed in the re-experience, and knowing what you know now, think about what might have been causing the "off" sensation.

John: There's no way to be sure. It's all so unclear. What if I'm just making it all up, and there was nothing to it at all?

Jane: Do you really believe that?

John: [pauses...] No. It was real, and it was "off." I just didn't pay attention to it.

Jane: I want you to stay with the 8-sense memory of your coworker's faces, and let the experience sink in. Just be with it for a while.

John: [quiet and thoughtful for more than a minute]

John: [quietly] Damn…

Jane: What?

John: I see it now. How could I not have seen it all along? God, how embarrassing. They were feeling sorry for me. My boss was right and I had it all backwards. I convinced myself that I was a hero but the reality was exactly as my boss said, and as my coworkers thought but didn't say.

That was the breakthrough. John and Jane continued their discussion for quite a while after that, using the 8-sense technique to look at quite a few aspects of John's experience with his boss, and a number of other experiences at other times in John's life. John discovered that he habitually distorted his perception of reality with a strong me-bias, which generated expectations that his unconscious mind confirmed (the confirmation bias), and which were reinforced with a lifelong habit of being self-referencing to the point that he rejected (unconsciously) the viewpoints of all others when they differed from his, and cast himself as the hero in his theater of the mind.

Ultimately, this new awareness enabled John to see his me-bias and consciously allow for other possibilities. Awareness didn't eliminate his me-bias, but it gave him a more balanced way to see himself in the context of his situation at work and in life, in a more objective way. And finally, after some 8-sense visualization, he was able to identify the trigger that launched his self-referencing personality habit. The trigger (which he could now use as an alert, warning him to change his way of thinking) was that same "off" feeling that he talked about with Jane. Ultimately, after some mental rehearsal and practice, he developed the habit of automatically seeing a broader range of possibilities and being more objective about them. He called it the habit of "openness."

Did you notice how resistant John was to any suggestion or hint that his perceptions might be wrong? He even believed that his boss was blind to the truth, and unable to see things as they actually were. John wasn't really resisting the truth, in fact he was trying hard to cooperate so that he could understand what went wrong with the experience with his boss. John sincerely believed that his view of the situation was the reality of it, and it felt to him like he was not clinging to his point of view, but actually defending the truth. He had no inkling that his perceptions might have been wrong, and that his job was in jeopardy. Internally it all felt so real, so genuine, so authentic, yet, as he came to realize, it was all manufactured by his faulty habits of mind.

When you try to penetrate your inner workings – your unconscious habits of mind – you can expect honestly and authentically to think and feel that your point of view (your "truth") is the actual reality. You can't help it; you're built that way. We all are. That's why it's so important to be the objective observer of yourself, and to consciously force yourself to understand other points of view, even if you believe them to be wrong. You don't have to agree with them, but you do need to understand them. The mere fact of admitting them into your awareness adds them into the mix of information available to your unconscious mind; your "WYSIATI". Your unconscious mind then does its thing (remember the coherence function?) by evaluating all the information available to it, and drawing the most compelling conclusion. In the example above, John's unconscious mind delivered a revised version of reality in the form of an "aha" moment accompanied by a sense of rightness. It was an "aha" that surprised and dismayed him, but it also had the ring of truth. His "aha" was reinforced by bodily sensations that always accompany his epiphanies – a physical feeling of relief and relaxation in his chest.

Your 8-sense exploration of your disappointing experiences will differ greatly from John's, but if you fully re-experience them (to bring forth all of the unconscious associations), if you are able to take an objective, third-party view of the experience, if you force yourself to understand other points-of-view (even if you don't believe them), if you pay attention to even the most subtle and unnoticed head, heart, and gut signals that were part of the experience, and finally if you stay open to all the possibilities (including the ones that don't feel good or seem wrong), then your unconscious mind will process it all, and as it was designed to do, it will come up with the right answers.

All you're really doing is getting out of your own way and letting your marvelous mind do what it was made to do.

ATTACHMENT C

The Repeating Question Technique – Peeling the Unconscious Onion

The Repeating Question technique is a way to get a deeper understanding of an idea, a meaningful event, an emotional reaction, an attitude, or any other experience. For our purposes, it's an excellent way to bring forth an understanding of what's going on in your unconscious mind.

The Technique

The process is what it says: you ask yourself a question, answer the question, then ask the same question about the answer you just gave. You continue repeating until you have a complete, conscious grasp of the experience. The process is simple, but rich with possibilities for deeper understanding.

It starts with a question such as, "Why was [the experience] so important, so meaningful?" You'll come up with easy, superficial answers quickly. Jot down key words to remind you of your thinking.

Then – and this is the key to getting to the heart of the matter – ask and answer the question, "Why is <u>that</u> [the reason you gave to the previous question] so important?" Again, jot down your answer(s). And do it again, again, and yet again until you reach a full understanding of the experience and its true meaning for you.

Continue "drilling down" with the repeating question until you sense that you have reached the heart of the matter. You'll feel it as some kind of "aha" or feeling of relief, a satisfaction, rather than a sense of wanting to stop or to move on to some other subject. If you feel stumped or blocked at any level of repeating questions, that's a sign that you're unconsciously avoiding something. You'll need to break through that unconscious resistance: push through it by re-asking the repeating question, and if necessary, speculating about answers that don't feel right for you, but might be true of others. Again, jot down the key words/phrases. At some point, you'll have that "aha" and you'll intuitively know that you've discovered what you were looking for. Occasionally, you may still find yourself blocked and unable to break through.

Sometimes, when you're blocked and can't think of an answer, it helps to use your imagination and make up an answer, or give an answer that you think could be true for someone else, even if it doesn't seem true for you. Because your imagination taps into your unconscious associations, it can pull important truths from the same place your unconscious habits of mind reside. When you explore these "pretend" answers, try to keep your mind open to possibilities, even possibilities you don't initially think are true for you. You can surprise yourself with breakthroughs and unexpected "aha" moments. There's no risk because you'll know as you explore whether or not the answer is true for you, and if it holds clues that make sense to pursue. The key, as you explore these "fictitious" answers is to be alert for emotional responses, especially strongly positive or negative reactions. If you experience anxiety, however faint it may be, and want to avoid further exploration of an answer, it may be a signal that it's important for you to continue that line of thought. And, of course, if you're strongly attracted to a line of thinking, you should pursue that. If the line of exploration "leaves you cold" and gives up no head, heart, or gut signals, it's probably a dead end. Go on to another line of inquiry.

Getting the Most from the Technique

When you select an event to examine, don't merely remember it, *re-experience* it. Use the 8-sense technique to relive it in your mind, including what happened, what you felt, and anything else you can recall about the experience like sights, sounds, tastes, smells, and sensations as well as thoughts, feelings, and emotions. Re-experience it in your mind's eye and get a sense of what made this activity so meaningful. Spend a few moments "getting into" the experience of the event.

Maybe you'll get to your "final answer" quickly, maybe it will take many repeating questions to get to it, but eventually you'll get down to a single word or short phrase that expresses the essence of why the experience was meaningful.

Example of the Repeating Questions Technique

To illustrate the use of the repeating question technique, we'll use the example of "Tom" and "Janet." Tom was trying to discover his Core Purpose (see Chapter 5). He chose to examine an event from his life that was particularly meaningful to him. In this event, he was the "hero" of a baseball game when he hit the game winning home run. The experience still resonates in him as highly meaningful – more so than you'd expect from a mere baseball game – and a clue to some of his inner motivation.

Janet: *So, Tom, which life event do you want to look at?*

Tom: *Let's try the baseball homerun one, when I was in college. For some reason, that one has always stayed with me. I replay it in my head all the time, and the good feelings about it never fade.*

Janet: *Good one. OK, let's take a minute or so to review it in your head. Re-live it as much as you can. Maybe you should close your eyes to help block out distractions?*

[Janet talks Tom through an 8-sense experience of the baseball game and the home run, asking him to recall people, place, what the day was like, what were the sights, sounds, feeling, emotions, and thoughts... any prompts that will bring the full richness of the experience back to Tom's mind.]

Tom: *Got it. I'm ready.*

Janet: Here we go. Tom, why was this event so meaningful for you?

Tom: Well, I was the hero. The spotlight was on me, and I felt great!

Janet: And why was <u>that</u> so meaningful for you?

Tom: We were the underdogs, but we showed everyone that we could really play a great game. We were better than they thought we were.

Janet: Why was <u>that</u> so meaningful?

Tom: I guess because I was the guy that made it happen. I felt good about myself. I actually felt powerful and competent.

Janet: Again, why was <u>that</u> so meaningful for you?

Tom: Well, it just was; I can't think of anything more about it.

Janet: [Pause...] Try again. Why was it so meaningful that you felt powerful and competent?

Tom: I can't think of anything else.

Janet: Try one more time. Be open to anything that comes up for you.

Tom: Still nothing. I'm stuck. Let's move on to something else.

Janet: Not just yet. Let's try a different tack. Try making something up. Use your imagination.

Tom: That's kind of foolish, isn't it?

Janet: Give it a try. What can it hurt? Make up anything.

Tom: Okay. This is really silly...I was making a contribution to world peace.

Janet: Yeah, you're right, that was silly, but stick with it anyway. Was there anything to this idea about contributing to world peace that resonates with you?

Tom: [Tom hesitates...then he says,] Well...yeah. Something about it felt good...satisfying. Not world peace of course, that really was far-fetched. But something about world peace made me think about happiness, and that made me think about my teammates' faces; they looked so happy. [Notice the chain of associations: world peace, happiness, teammate's faces. There were undoubtedly other associations that didn't rise to Tom's consciousness awareness.]

Janet: Okay, let's go with that. Why were your teammate's happy faces meaningful for you?

Tom: Hmm. [Tom thinks quietly for a moment.] It felt good that I made everyone else happier and that they felt better about themselves for a while.

Janet: And why was it so meaningful for you to make everyone else happier and feel better?

Tom: Because, even though it was only for a little while, everybody's life was a little bit better, and I made it happen.

Janet: Why was _that_ meaningful for you?

Tom: It just was. I don't think we have to go any further; this feels like "it" in my gut.

Janet: Say it one more time to be sure.

Tom: This event was meaningful because I helped some people make a bit of their lives better. Yeah. That's it.

Janet: *Let me ask you a "reality check" question before we go on to the next life event. There are different levels of needs, you know, safety and security needs, esteem needs, and some others?*

Tom: *Sure. What about them?*

Janet: *Well, maybe this event was all about social needs. Your home run made you a more important member of the team. Or maybe it was about self-esteem. You felt good about being the hero, and for a while your self-esteem must have been sky high. What's the real bottom line for you in this event?*

Tom: *Huh. ... Lemme think for a second. Both of the things you said are true. My self-esteem couldn't have been higher, and never before or since, did I feel more like a central and important part of the team. But what I remember most, and what to this day still makes me feel good, is the happiness I saw in my teammates. That's where the gratification was. And that's why I picked it as a meaningful event in my life, otherwise, it was just a baseball game.*

Janet: *Good job, Tom. I wrote down key words as we were doing the repeating questions, and I circled "made their lives better" as the core idea. Let me get out a new sheet of paper for the next one. Are you ready to move on to another life event?*

This technique can be done alone or with a trusted person to coach you. If you try it on your own, don't let yourself off the hook if you stall out for a round or two of the repeating question. Use your imagination if you have to. Keep drilling down until you reach the most basic answer.

ATTACHMENT D

My Top Ten List of the Best Books for Non-Scientists about Mind/Brain Science

Thinking, Fast and Slow
Daniel Kahneman (Nobel Prize laureate)
2011 ISBN: 978-0-374-27563-1

Subliminal
How Your Unconscious Mind Rules Your Behavior
Leonard Mlodinow
2012 ISBN: 978-0-307-37821-7

Incognito
The Secret Lives of the Brain
David Eagleman
2011 ISBN: 978-0-307-38992-3

Born to Believe
God, Science and the Origin of Ordinary and Extraordinary Beliefs
Andrew Newberg, MD and Mark Robert Waldman
2006 ISBN: 978-0-7432-7498

Blink
The Power of Thinking Without Thinking
Malcolm Gladwell
2005 ISBN: 0-316-17232-4

The Highest Goal
The Secret that Sustains You in Every Moment
Michael Ray
2004 ISBN: 1-57675-286-0

Creativity in Business
Michael Ray and Rochelle Myers
1986 ISBN: 0-385-24851-2

A Technique for Producing Ideas
James Webb Young
1940 [This is an old book. It predates the ISBN numbering system.]

Brainwashed
The Seductive Appeal of Mindless Neuroscience
Sally Satel and Scott O. Lilienfeld
2013 ISBN: 978-0-465-01877-2

Understanding Complexity
[Not about the mind/brain specifically, but helps understand how
the mind could be an 'emergent property' of the brain. The book
is a summary of a course of instruction provided by The Teaching
Company]
Professor Scott E. Page
2009 ISBN: 1-59803-560-6

ATTACHMENT E

About the Author

My full name is Errol Dean Alexander. If we ever meet, call me Alex.

My adult life started on my eighteenth birthday, the day I enlisted in the US Army. I made the rank of sergeant as a nineteen year old tank commander in Germany, went to West Point for four years, and (after graduation with a bachelor's degree in engineering) had a brief but successful military career, including two years in wartime Viet Nam, where I earned three Bronze Stars, two Purple Hearts, and the rank of Captain in the Armored Cavalry. At various times in the Army I also earned the coveted Airborne wings, qualified as an Army Ranger, was awarded the Combat Infantryman's Badge, and received a Top Secret security rating from the US government.

After military service, I made the transition into business by graduating from Harvard Business School with an MBA degree in marketing and finance. I started my business career as a management consultant, went into banking for a dozen years, and then went back to consulting for another ten. I have held management positions with Crocker Bank (now Wells Fargo), American Express, and the Stanford Research Institute, as well as consulting projects for the likes of Charles Schwab, Monsanto, the United States Federal Reserve Bank, Fujitsu (Japan), ANZ Bank (Australia), the U.S. Army, and many startups and small businesses with names you wouldn't recognize. My titles have included CEO (three times), SVP Corporate Development, VP Marketing, and others.

My career – and my sense of purpose in life – changed dramatically in 1995 when I joined Michael Gerber's E-Myth Academy (now E-Myth Worldwide) and at last found my passion in the field of small business development. While at EMW, I was responsible for the creation and writing of Gerber's E-Myth Mastery Program, at that time the world's most innovative and comprehensive small business coaching system. I also made major contributions to the creation of EMW's worldwide network of coaches.

In 2000, after completing the E-Myth Mastery Program, I left the E-Myth Academy for academia. I continued my leading-edge research and development of business management and leadership practices while teaching Strategic Management, Business Basics, and Leadership at Menlo College and Santa Clara University, both in California's "Silicon Valley."

Academia wasn't real-world enough, so in 2005 I returned to the *very* real world of small business development. I recruited a team of 14 master coaches, raised the necessary seed money, and founded the Alliance for Enterprise Leadership, Inc., (doing business as the Full Spectrum Coaching Company, initially in the USA and Australia). This put me seriously back into the world of small business coaching. My first task was to develop a completely new, up-to-the-minute and comprehensive business coaching system, which we call the Full Spectrum Business Development Program. That task took five years to complete, but it was worth it because the Full Spectrum program, based on what our clients tell us, is the very best available today. We're also at the leading edge of business education, having this year (in cooperation with Australia's GEM International College of Business), launched the Full Spectrum Academy, which offers you an on-line, fully accredited Diploma of Business Management. You can earn your diploma on-line, at your own speed and at any location, for less than a third of the cost of a conventional business diploma. If you're interested, you can learn about Full Spectrum Coaching at www.fullspectrumcoach.com, and about the Full Spectrum Academy and its fully accredited business management diploma at www.fullspectrumacademy.com.

I'm currently dividing my time between the demands of being the Founder, Chairman of the Board, and CEO of the Full Spectrum Businesses, and writing books on entrepreneurship and leadership.

Made in the USA
Middletown, DE
26 January 2016